Praise for *Out of Sight*

"For years, Eisnitz has been a courageous and eloquent champion for the millions of suffering animals in 'factory farms' who can't speak for themselves. In this new book she shares the information she has gathered and combines this with her own personal and deeply moving memoir. Shocking, heartbreaking, and full of compassion, this will reach into your heart, make you think about what you eat, and inspire you to do your bit to make this a more caring world."

—Dr. Jane Goodall DBE, founder of the
Jane Goodall Institute and UN Messenger of Peace

"In *Out of Sight*, Gail Eisnitz weaves together two narratives: how she shut down horrific cruelty inflicted on farmed animals in America, and how she discovered the cause of her abnormal vision and her occasional and unpredictable sense of detachment from the activities she was engaged in. In combination, they make an inspiring story of how one person can overcome obstacles, both external and internal, to contribute to making the world a better place."

—Peter Singer, co-founder of The Life You Can Save and
author of *Animal Liberation* and *Consider the Turkey*

"This riveting book is a testament to one woman's courage and tenacity in the face of powerful and corrupt business interests, crippling health issues, and jaw-dropping animal abuse. If you wish to eat like you give a damn, read this book."

—Jonathan Balcombe, PhD, *New York Times* bestselling
author of *What a Fish Knows*

"*Out of Sight* is a deep and unflinching look at the cruel treatments suffered by animals killed for meat and by the workers doing the killing and processing. No one who reads this book will ever again see a piece of meat as just a piece of meat. You will forever understand that meat is just the last stop on a journey of suffering."

—Carl Safina, *New York Times* bestselling author of *Beyond Words: What Animals Think and Feel* and *Alfie and Me: What Owls Know, What Humans Believe*

"Absolutely stunning! Gail Eisnitz's fascinating life experiences reveal odd (and sometimes evil) goings-on in surprising places, from hospitals to pig farms. An eye- and mind-opening read from someone who has been there, found things out, and ripped back the curtain so that we can know all about them, too."

—Ingrid Newkirk, founder and president of PETA and author of *Free the Animals, One Can Make a Difference*, and *Animalkind*

"*Out of Sight* is a brave, important, and inspiring book that deserves a broad global audience. Gail Eisnitz has been indefatigable in her efforts on behalf of the powerless and voiceless, those animal beings—so-called 'food animals'—whose horrific lives are hidden from view. Her new book is a testament to one woman's unwavering empathy and strength in the face of profound obstacles. A truly stirring account of endurance and triumph for everyone who cares deeply about animals and their wellbeing."

—Marc Bekoff, PhD, author of *The Emotional Lives of Animals: A Leading Scientist Explores Animal Joy, Sorrow, and Empathy—and Why They Matter*

"A light in the darkness of institutional animal abuse, Gail Eisnitz has been relentless in her efforts to make cruelty visible and accountable. This engrossing memoir tells the story of her decades as an investigative journalist, including the terrible personal adversity she endured while trying to expose injustice and relieve the suffering of other creatures. Eisnitz is a writer of great skill and enormous compassion, a truly heroic woman, and shows us in *Out of Sight* how we too can be a force for good."
—Matthew Scully, author of *Dominion* and *Fear Factories*

"Gail Eisnitz's efforts on behalf of farm animals are to be commended, and her memoir detailing those efforts is both disturbing and inspiring. I am hopeful that this eye-opening examination of meat-industry practices leads to meaningful reforms. I will continue to work in Congress to improve emergency and disaster preparedness for farm animals as a way to both ensure their humane treatment and to save hundreds of millions of dollars in taxpayer dollars spent to indemnify farmers and ranchers for often careless livestock losses."
—Congressman Steve Cohen (D-TN), longtime member of the Congressional Animal Protection Caucus

"Gail Eisnitz is a riveting, best-informed writer about the meat industry. Her remarkable previous book, *Slaughterhouse*, is mandatory reading at Friends of Animals. This new book delivers the most compelling reasons to be vegan, and to understand that the enormous cruelty inside the meat industry can't be mitigated. We simply must stop seeing animals as our food."
—Priscilla Feral, president of Friends of Animals

Out of Sight

An Undercover Investigator's Fight for Animal Rights and Her Own Survival

GAIL A. EISNITZ

Skyhorse Publishing

Copyright © 2025 by Gail A. Eisnitz

All rights reserved. No part of this book may be reproduced in any manner without the express written consent of the publisher, except in the case of brief excerpts in critical reviews or articles. All inquiries should be addressed to Skyhorse Publishing, 307 West 36th Street, 11th Floor, New York, NY 10018.

Skyhorse Publishing books may be purchased in bulk at special discounts for sales promotion, corporate gifts, fund-raising, or educational purposes. Special editions can also be created to specifications. For details, contact the Special Sales Department, Skyhorse Publishing, 307 West 36th Street, 11th Floor, New York, NY 10018 or info@skyhorsepublishing.com.

Skyhorse® and Skyhorse Publishing® are registered trademarks of Skyhorse Publishing, Inc.®, a Delaware corporation.

Visit our website at www.skyhorsepublishing.com.
Please follow our publisher Tony Lyons on Instagram @tonylyonsisuncertain.

10 9 8 7 6 5 4 3 2 1

Library of Congress Cataloging-in-Publication Data is available on file.

Cover design by David Ter-Avanesyan

Print ISBN: 978-1-5107-8233-4
Ebook ISBN: 978-1-5107-8238-9

Printed in the United States of America

For Jessica, Asher, Amanda, and Zia—the future.

Contents

Author's Note		xi
Introduction		xiii
Part One:	A World Made Up of Dots	1
Part Two:	A Fortress Around My Heart	33
Part Three:	Animal Activist on the Loose	75
Part Four:	Giving Voice to the Voiceless	99
Part Five:	By Sheer Power of Will	129
Part Six:	No Milk of Human Kindness	163
Part Seven:	A Prosecutor Steps to the Plate	183
Part Eight:	Connecting the Dots	203
Part Nine:	The Meat Industry's Free Pass	219
Part Ten:	A Tearful Goodbye	227
Afterword: A Heartfelt Plea		237
Acknowledgments		243
Endnotes		245

Author's Note

This memoir is a truthful recollection of actual events in the author's life. Some conversations have been recreated and/or supplemented. The names and details of some individuals have been changed to respect their privacy.

Introduction

For most of my life, I thought I was crazy.

In my memory, it began one night when I was eight years old. I simply *thought* of the word *hell*. The word was intolerable to me—evil, profane, a self-fulfilling prophecy, synonymous with death in my young brain. I believed that if I repeated other "hell-like" words over and over in my head for hours—*Helen . . . help us . . . help us . . . hello . . . Helen . . . help us . . . help us . . . hello . . . Helen . . . help us . . . help us . . . hello . . .*—I could magically neutralize the word *hell* and the potential doom it represented to me. If it wasn't the word *hell*, maybe I wouldn't go there for thinking it.

It was just one of thousands of such rituals—now psychologists call them "compulsions"—that I engaged in during my childhood, teenage, and adult years. My fear of profanity and offending God was just one of many classic symptoms of the anxiety disease obsessive compulsive disorder (OCD). And sadly, although I was in the relentless grip of this bizarre illness in all my waking moments, I wouldn't hear the term *obsessive compulsive disorder* for more than thirty years.

OCD was the first of two psychological/neurological conditions that would hijack my body, brain, and my very being. These disorders would cause me to understand the true meaning of isolation and alienation and would ultimately propel me to spend my life speaking out for the most isolated and alienated among us: farm animals.

Only after decades of struggling with invisible demons would a bigger picture emerge. The pieces of an enormous puzzle would finally come together, creating a mosaic of experiences that would ultimately affect the lives of millions of animals and fill me with a sense of wholeness and self-acceptance and a peace of mind beyond my wildest expectations.

Part One

A World Made Up of Dots

Chapter 1

I donned a long paper gown. It was a pale-yellow color with narrow paper strings that tied around the neck and waist. I put on blue latex gloves, too. Visitors had to be covered from head to toe; *Methicillin-resistant Staphylococcus aureus*—a bacterium otherwise known as MRSA—can be a killer.

The patient in front of me did not look familiar—I had not seen Tim in a few years. Although I talked to him on the phone weekly, now he was barely recognizable; the breathing tube in his mouth led to a ventilator and obstructed part of his face. Machines around him were intimidatingly whirring and beeping as they kept him alive and monitored his vitals. At seventy-three, he still had a full shock of dark-brown hair and a scruffy auburn beard. He had been sedated and was sleeping soundly, unaware that I had traveled eight hundred miles to see him. That was okay with me. I just didn't want him to die alone.

I had known Timothy Walker, Navy veteran, U.S. Department of Agriculture (USDA) whistleblower, humanitarian, and all-around good guy for nearly thirty years when he disappeared in May 2018.

It wasn't the first time Tim had vanished. He'd gone missing once before, back in 2016. After retirement from the USDA, Tim had become a loner. Other than me, he didn't really seem to have friends. He had siblings who lived halfway across the country, but friends—not so much. Tim had two very modest homes—a small duplex in Daytona and a humble house in Naples, Florida.

Tim hadn't returned my calls in weeks, and, being an investigator, I decided to do some detective work. I contacted the police, who then went to his homes and reported back that everything looked in order. I phoned all the hospitals in both towns, as well as three Veterans Administration facilities. The VA social worker I spoke with in Naples was rude and uncaring. "Did it ever occur to you that maybe he doesn't want to be found?" she asked tersely.

I was stunned. "No, ma'am," I said. "Maybe some veterans don't want to be found, but not Tim." Tim and I were best buds. He would never willingly desert me.

When I'd last spoken with Tim weeks earlier, he had been heading from Florida to Missouri to briefly visit family, but that's where the trail had gone cold. I only learned what had happened to him five months later, when he phoned me out of the blue. I was shocked and immensely relieved to hear his voice. He explained that while visiting family in St. Louis, he'd suffered a stroke. He'd been hospitalized and then stayed with his brother John in Missouri for some time, until John drove him back to his little duplex in Daytona. When he resurfaced five months later, I insisted that he give me contact information for John, if he ever vanished again.

And missing again he went. It was spring 2018, and weeks passed with no contact from Tim. Again, I worked the phones, calling hospitals in Daytona and Naples. The last one I called in Naples had a Tim Walker registered as a patient. It was *my* Tim.

A devout Catholic, Tim had apparently collapsed in church one Saturday afternoon and had been rushed by ambulance to the hospital. After locating him, I contacted his brother John, who was grateful to learn of Tim's whereabouts. A chain smoker for almost sixty years, Tim had serious circulatory problems, including neuropathy in his lower extremities, and a surgeon had attempted, to my understanding, to graft an artery in his leg to improve blood flow. In subsequent weeks, the patient would nearly bleed to death. Tim would be shuttled among a series of nursing homes and hospitals. It would take more telephone work to follow his trail.

"It's a nonsurvivable wound." I will never forget those words. That was the term the hospitalist uttered into the phone when describing the area of Tim's

A World Made Up of Dots

leg where the surgeon had attempted to graft the artery. A *nonsurvivable wound*? How can one have a nonsurvivable wound? But Tim apparently did.

He also had *Methicillin-resistant Staphylococcus aureus.*

I didn't know if his brother John was going to make the trip from St. Louis to Naples. I didn't want Tim, the man who had singlehandedly changed the trajectory of my life, to spend his remaining days on Earth alone.

That's what brought me from Asheville to Naples, to see my dying friend.

Chapter 2

My friendship with Tim had begun in 1989 with a somewhat anonymous letter I'd received while working as a field investigator at the Washington, DC-based Humane Society of the United States. Cows, the letter said, hanging upside down from the bleed rail at Kaplan Industries, Florida's largest slaughterhouse, were being skinned while they were still fully conscious. The writer explained that it was not only cruel to the poor animals who were struggling frantically and bellowing, but it posed a serious danger to the "head skinners" and "leggers" who were stationed below.

"I have contacted a number of federal agencies but have been told there is nothing they can do," read the letter. "They also told me that the problems I described exist all over the country, that they are just a little worse at Kaplan's." Although the letter was unsigned, the writer had taken care to print his return address on the front of the envelope. Using that address, I was able to track down the source of the letter.

Tim Walker, then forty-three, I would learn, was employed as a bovine brucellosis tester for the U.S. Department of Agriculture. (Brucellosis is a highly contagious disease which causes abortions in cows and posed a financial threat to Florida's beef industry.) It was not Tim's dream job. He had left his hometown in Missouri a year earlier bound for Florida with the promise of working as a federal animal health technician. He had long dreamed of a job helping animals; little did he know he would find himself on a catwalk in a slaughterhouse blood pit taking samples from cows who were *supposed* to be dead.

I couldn't have known at the time that Tim's letter would launch me on a grueling odyssey that would take me into the dark recesses of a world most people never see or even think about. Over the next thirteen years, I would document slaughterhouse atrocities on video and in affidavits with plant workers and federal meat inspectors who had spent a combined total of 3 million hours on the kill floor. My investigation would expose corruption at the highest levels of the U.S. Department of Agriculture and an incestuous relationship and revolving door between that agency and the meat companies it is supposed to regulate. It would shed light on an industry that intentionally promotes a production mentality where high-speed slaughter lines are not to stop for anything—not for injured workers, not for contaminated meat, and least of all, not for slow, uncooperative, or disabled animals.

My investigation would reveal unimaginable cruelty to animals inside USDA-inspected slaughterhouses across the country. And it would culminate in publication of my book *Slaughterhouse: The Shocking Story of Greed, Neglect, and Inhumane Treatment Inside the U.S. Meat Industry* and in a front-page story in *The Washington Post* exposing my findings. That story would generate outrage among members of Congress who would then appropriate tens of millions of dollars in funding for enforcement of the federal Humane Methods of Slaughter Act (HMSA). At the time, that law, which grants USDA meat inspectors authority to enforce humane regulations in slaughterhouses, had been on the books for forty-three years. It had been "zero budgeted"—meaning no monies had ever been allocated to enforce it—since its enactment.

Chapter 3

My world has always been pixelated—like static on an old analog television, or the pointillism of French post-impressionistic painter Georges Seurat. In darkness, the dots are more prominent and cause my whole world to shimmer. "Mommy, why is the world made up of dots?" I asked often, as far back as I can remember.

My curious Mom didn't know how to respond. That was okay; it wasn't a big deal to me, although I was surprised to eventually learn that nobody else saw dots. Plus, I didn't recognize colors the way most of my friends did; although uncommon in females, I was also red-green colorblind. Between the dots and the colorblindness, I had my own special way of perceiving the world.

Every day my sister, Lisa, and I would walk "the path"—a Little Red Riding Hood–type trail through the deep Whippany, New Jersey, woods—from home to Salem Drive Elementary School. After class, we would return home and play with the neighborhood kids as we followed what we believed were ancient "Indian trails" through the forested half-acre wonderland that was our backyard. A pile of boulders with a birch tree growing between the rocks became our own private island; a tunnel through snow was an igloo; a cardboard box propped up by a stick with a string and a carrot was a rabbit trap. We skated on frozen puddles, played cops and robbers, hide and seek.

One evening, when I was fourteen, I happened to stumble upon a Public Broadcasting System television documentary sponsored by the Quaker Oats Company. The name of the show was *Say Goodbye*.[1] The program was about the destruction of wildlife; a "memorial to the animals of the earth."

During the broadcast, a camera operator in the Arctic zoomed in on some figures moving swiftly across an ice floe. A mother polar bear and her two cubs were frantically fleeing—steam emanating from their mouths, sea water splashing—as a helicopter above the barren, snow-draped landscape chased them down.

Suddenly, out of nowhere, a hunter appeared on the icy ground, raising his rifle and shooting at the mother bear. She took a direct hit. In the documentary's next frame, the mother, moaning pitifully, barely able to hold her head up, looked back at her little cubs.

Frightened by the hunter, the cubs scurried off, turning once to peer back at their dying mom—the two puffballs of pure white, their glossy black noses pointed downward, their huge brown eyes stared, puzzled, directly into the camera's lens.

Their mother was dying, and the cubs, too small to fend for themselves, wouldn't survive. Their faces were fraught with abject terror and, even more disturbing, total bewilderment. It was the documentary's closing image.

My fate was sealed. So powerful was the image of the polar bear cubs that it became embedded in my brain. To say that it was a turning point in my life would be an understatement.

Shortly after the documentary aired, I was assigned to write a high school research paper on a topic of my choice. I selected the issue of threatened and endangered species. I would learn that the passenger pigeon, which I featured in my paper, once so abundant in the United States that flocks would blacken the skies for miles, had been three to five *billion* birds strong. Now it was extinct. Unchecked hunting combined with loss of habitat spelled the death knell for a creature that had at one time been the most plentiful bird species on earth.

Likewise, the colorful Carolina parakeet, the only parrot indigenous to the eastern United States, had been exterminated by farmers who deemed it a "pest," by deforestation for agricultural lands, and by those who hunted it for its plumage to adorn ladies' hats.

Today, around 1 million animal and plant species worldwide—including one out of four of the earth's mammals—are threatened with extinction.[2,3]

The polar bear is on that list.

Chapter 4

It was the first junior varsity basketball home game of the season, the small private school I attended in Morristown, New Jersey, against another preparatory school about twenty miles away. We'd been practicing for weeks. I was relief point guard—a terrible player—I had never been very athletically inclined.

I was on the sidelines. The crowd seated on the bleachers on the west side of the gymnasium was cheering, the basketball whizzed from one player to the next. Score! The opposing team made a basket. My team raced down the court. Score! It was a very close game; we were down 58–52 when Coach Daniels, probably out of pity, put me in the game to play out the fourth quarter.

I took my position on the court, waiting for the ball to come my way when, all of a sudden, I felt like I was in a dream. The detail and the vivid colors of the crowd in the bleachers, the basketball hoops, the striations and game lines on the gymnasium floor, the swift movements of the players, and the diffuse lighting coming from fixtures suspended from the rafters, all conspired to overwhelm my senses. My brain became foggy, nothing seemed real, and the room started to spin. I could no longer see what I was doing, where I was going. I was gripped with terror.

Panicked, I somehow held it together and stayed on the court as the scoreboard clock ticked down—an interminable and agonizing ten minutes—until the final buzzer sounded.

I was reminded of the two abandoned polar bear cubs on the snowy ice floe who, since I'd watched the PBS documentary a year earlier, were indelibly imprinted on my psyche. Like them, I, too, was momentarily frozen—stricken with fear and confusion. Not knowing what was happening or where to turn, I felt vulnerable and petrified. And, most of all, I felt alone.

Of course, it wasn't the first time that my surroundings had gotten jumbled, that my environment hadn't made sense to me, that my brain felt bombarded with extraneous details. It had happened before, just not in an exposed setting like the center of a basketball court in front of scores of cheering fans. Confusion was actually a constant companion; it would, for instance, overtake me in the shoe department at Epstein's, a large retail store in downtown Morristown. As I entered that department, my eyes, or more aptly, my brain, would be hijacked by the fluorescent lighting and the mishmash of shoes. My depth perception impaired, a sense of unreality would set in. I was eleven years old. I thought I was losing my mind.

Later, it happened when quietly hiking in the woods. In the forest, where my eyes were barraged by a tangle of mottled tree trunks, branches, verdant leaves, and pine needles—all competing for my attention—I was essentially immobilized by too much visual detail. Barely able to put one foot in front of the other, I quite literally couldn't see the forest for the trees.

I had never voiced my fears about this recurring problem; instinct told me to keep them to myself. It was my secret. But, after the high school basketball game, I shared with my mother what had happened to me and how terrified I was. My mom scheduled an appointment for me with our family physician, who ordered an electroencephalogram or EEG. At age fifteen, I felt like a freak—or Dr. Frankenstein for that matter—lying on a hospital exam table and having electrodes affixed to my head.

The results of the EEG were unremarkable, and the issue was shelved. My symptoms were chalked up to anxiety.

With no definitive diagnosis or further discussion, and unable to determine the source of my symptoms, I got it into my befuddled brain that I alone was responsible for—somehow causing—my visual overload. That *I* was the problem, that *I* was to blame. *Why am I doing this to myself?* I interrogated myself every time my symptoms surfaced. Both a question and an accusation, it became a menacing mantra in my head. With that refrain—*Why am I doing this to myself?*—I had dangerously dipped my toe into a turbulent and unforgiving sea of shame and self-contempt.

Chapter 5

I had pounded the pavement in Washington, DC, after graduating from the School of Agriculture and Environmental Sciences at Rutgers University in New Jersey with a degree in Natural Resource Conservation. All I wanted to do was to "save animals"—to be hired by a national conservation or animal welfare organization. It was the early 1980s, animal protection was a fledgling movement, and I was unable to convince any such organization to take a chance on me.

At the same time, I discovered a hidden talent—drawing—and began illustrating threatened and endangered species. My obsessively detailed renderings were painstakingly drawn with dots—again, enter painter Georges Seurat—much as I see the world in a pixelated fashion, and my medium was fine point felt-tip pens. My illustrations accompanied newspaper and magazine articles that I wrote on the issue, appeared in animal protection publications and field guides, and even hung in a one-woman exhibit in the New Jersey State Museum, Trenton. I worked maniacally, drawing and trying to bring attention to the plight of threatened and endangered wildlife. At the time, I was living in a rental house in northern New Jersey with three women friends—I was twenty-six years old.

One February night, I was putting the finishing touches on a series of animal illustrations for a third-grade science textbook. I'd been working on the project for weeks and it was due the next day. I was drawing feverishly when the phone rang. It was my mother. I needed to come home right away. Dad had gone missing.

I anxiously drove the thirty-five minutes to my parents' house. It was a clear and bitterly cold night. I parked the car at the top of the circular driveway, walked through the front door, and I could see that there were two uniformed police officers in the kitchen with Mom.

As it turned out, Mom and Dad had had an argument. That was nothing new. Their relationship, as far back as I could remember, had been extremely volatile; their fighting had been a constant in my life. This time, however, things had taken a turn for the worse; Dad had downed a bottle of sleeping pills and had driven off. Nobody knew where he was.

Dad's phone call came in on my parents' one-extension business line, a phone sitting on the kitchen desk. Mom and I would take turns talking with him: Mom somewhat detached when speaking with him; me, listening, persuading, pleading with him to give up his whereabouts. The police stood by—handcuffs, radios, holstered pistols hanging from their duty belts. For some inexplicable reason, they were not able to get the phone call traced.

Each time Mom had the receiver in hand, I sat at the kitchen table, my fingers entwined, awaiting my turn to talk. While most of my OCD rituals had long ago gone underground—they were still intrusive in my life, but I had, over the years, learned to mask them to the outside world—this time the stakes were too high; I couldn't stop myself. I engaged in a spectrum of compulsions—tapping, squinting, gritting—designed by my anxious brain to calm myself and to magically protect Dad.

Every time I spoke with Dad, he sounded more worn down, tired, sleepy. There were long pauses during which I was afraid we were losing him. At two hours and forty-five minutes into the call, he "reassured" me that, after he was gone, he would be "watching over me from above." Not the words of the stern, unsentimental, demanding man that was my dad.

For three excruciating hours, we kept Dad awake and talking on the line.

At two o'clock in the morning, after I'd waged an exhausting campaign begging him to tell me where he was, Dad caved. He told me he was cloistered away in a motel room at the Howard Johnson's just off of Route 10 in Whippany. He was about five miles from home, as the crow flies.

A World Made Up of Dots   15

Mom would stay behind on the phone with Dad, believing that her presence at the motel would incite him further. The decision was made that I would go with the police to find him. The two men jumped into the patrol car's front seat, and I flew into the back, a steel cage with bulletproof glass separating us. No lights, no sirens—at two o'clock in the morning there was no traffic. My expectation was crystalline: we would find Dad at the motel, get him into the squad car, and bring him home safely, where he belonged.

At the motel, there was an ambulance idling in the parking lot under a streetlight, two emergency medical technicians, bundled in ski jackets, standing outside, their breaths turning to steam in the frigid morning air. Exhaust billowed in small clouds from the vehicle's tailpipe. Call it denial, but my brain couldn't comprehend what they were doing there.

Dad had registered under his own name—and the officers and I made a mad dash down the stark hallway. "Go ahead, knock on the door," the officers told me. Dad would be less likely to answer if, looking through the peephole, he saw two burly law enforcers. The cops hung back, and then, somehow, they seemed to disappear into thin air.

I knocked. I heard some sounds—perhaps he was still on the phone with Mom. "Dad, it's me. Open up!" I waited; my heart pounding loudly in my ears as the blood coursed through my veins. There was a stirring in the room, movement. I knocked once more. "It's me, Dad. It's Gail. Open up!" I shouted.

It seemed like forever, but finally, the door opened a crack . . . and then a bit more. And suddenly, there he was: my father, the tall and intensely private man, the imposing, frightening authority-figure, standing now noticeably thin and wobbly before me in his boxer shorts and undershirt.

I opened the door further and squeezed into the room's small entryway. Dad teetered between me and the adjacent bathroom. And then, as if in slow motion, my father's body gave way, crumbling right before my eyes. I reacted swiftly. As my dad collapsed backwards in my direction, I somehow wedged my forearms under him, supporting him as best I could as I struggled to carefully lower what felt like dead weight to the carpeted floor.

In an instant, his eyes rolled back into his head.

Chapter 6

Crouching on the floor with Dad in my arms, I repeatedly shouted—screamed—for help. I was panic-stricken; I didn't want my father to die in my arms. What had happened to the two police officers? Where were the ambulance medics who had been stationed in the back parking lot? It seemed an eternity before the EMTs rushed into the room, the cops hanging back by the door.

Once inside, emergency personnel took over from me. One man felt for a pulse as the other lifted my father's eyelids, shined a flashlight into his eyes. Lying unconscious on the floor in his underwear, Dad looked unusually pale and thin, and *oh-so vulnerable*. His rib cage—outlined through his sleeveless white undershirt—protruded above a deeply sunken waist. The EMTs yanked the tank top from my dad's torso and administered an electric current through a paddle to his chest.

A package of Chuckles candies, wrapped five colorful flavors to a cellophane pack—like a circus tent—sat atop the motel dresser adjacent to the television. In his drugged state, Dad hadn't brought Chuckles with him to the motel. Was this Howard Johnson's brand of hospitality mint? Was it a cosmic joke? It was a moment of irony in a life-and-death situation.

After applying the electric current, the paramedics rolled a gurney in and lowered it to the floor; they lifted Dad onto it and transported him to the ambulance in the frigid morning air, a full moon lighting the motel parking lot. The patrol car—me again on the smooth vinyl back seat—followed the ambulance to Morristown Memorial, the hospital about a fifteen-minute drive away.

When we arrived at the hospital, to my surprise, my mother was waiting in the emergency room. A doctor and nurse outside the examining room, preparing to pump my father's stomach, permitted Mom and me inside to see him. Lying on the stretcher under a blanket in the examining room, a glass wall separating Dad from the ER's bustle, my father looked so tragically alone.

As Mom and I entered the examining room, Dad, now conscious, didn't seem to notice me. It was like I was invisible. Instead, he looked directly at my mother with doleful brown puppy-dog eyes.

"I'm so sorry, Phyllis," he said with deliberation.

I wanted to rush to his side and put my arms around him and tell him that it would all be okay. More importantly, I wanted Mom to do that. I wanted her to say, "I'm so sorry, Gerald. I'm just so grateful that you're alive." After what Dad had just endured, I wanted Mom to apologize to *him*.

But she didn't. She did not react—did not say a word. There was dead silence—the most deafening silence that I'd ever heard.

I spent the rest of the morning—after Dad was admitted to the psych ward for evaluation—at my parents' house with Mom, wanting to be sure that *she* was okay. I then drove the thirty-five minutes back to my rental house to hurriedly finish my illustrations for the science textbook due that morning.

Unable to make my deadline that day, I called my editor at the publishing house to tell him that the project would be a day late. "My dad had a heart attack last night," I fudged, "but he's going to be okay."

Chapter 7

That summer, I left the house one morning bound for a meeting in New York City. Because I knew that the landlord had hired an exterminator to spray the house that day, I left a sign on my bedroom door. In big purple letters I wrote: "MR. EXTERMINATOR: DO NOT SPRAY MY BEDROOM, I AM VIOLENTLY ALLERGIC TO PESTICIDES." Being conscious of the hazards of some chemicals, I chose to personally deal with any ants that came my way. That usually meant taking them to the nearest door to set them free.

Among the items leaning against one of my bedroom walls that morning was an illustration I had just completed of a two-week old bald eagle. It was to accompany a story I'd written for *New Jersey Audubon*—a birdwatchers' magazine. Since 1982 marked the bicentennial of the designation of the bald eagle as the symbol of freedom in the United States, I thought it was appropriate to profile the bird and its critically endangered status in New Jersey. A considerable amount of time and research had gone into the article and illustration.

When I returned home later that afternoon, I was devastated to find little rivulets of insecticide trickling down the eagle chick's face. Ignoring my note, the exterminator had entered my room and had sprayed his chemicals right over my drawing.

In despair, I phoned my mom who instructed me to leave the house—she didn't want me exposed to toxic chemicals. I drove to my parents' home. And I complained to my mom about the destruction of my eaglet. Mom's sage advice: write about it.

A World Made Up of Dots 19

And write about it I did. I wrote an essay comparing the destruction of my bald eaglet illustration from pesticides to the decimation of New Jersey's bald eagle population from DDT.

"The exterminator had sprayed the eagle illustration," I wrote, "senselessly destroying the baby eagle with his poison. The twinkle in the raptor's eyes had been replaced by tears, and golden-brown ink trickled over its face and through its downy breast. The soft, pink tongue no longer poked out from a laughing bill, but instead dribbled along the lower mandible and meandered over the edge."

At the time of my writing, the entire New Jersey bald eagle population had dwindled down to a single pair of raptors. Although unable to reproduce, they had remained faithful to New Jersey, coming back year after year to nest atop a Cumberland County pine tree. "DDT or other toxic contaminants are probably responsible for the reproductive failure of New Jersey's sole nesting pair," I wrote.

Wildlife biologists had, a few months earlier, placed a fifteen-day-old captive-born male chick in the pair's nest in the hopes that the adults would accept the eaglet as their own and raise him, and that he would return in about four years, when he matured, to breed in New Jersey.

"Since that time," I wrote, "I have seen photographs of the Cumberland County eaglet, who, at two weeks, looked strikingly similar to my exterminated creation. Things are going well for that character. And at ten pounds he is already larger than his surrogate parents.

"He will fly south later this year, and it is hoped that he will not encounter toxic contaminants that are still used extensively in Central and South America. He is expected to return to his Cumberland County home someday, and with him bring generations of eagles back to New Jersey.

"That gawky creature learning to fly from a Cumberland County treetop carries the future of New Jersey's bald eagles on his wings, alone."

And the rest is history. For, unlike most endangered species, that immature bird of prey fulfilled his promise, bringing generations of eagle descendants back to the state. New Jersey's bald eagle population did indeed rebound—it has soared, in fact—to a resounding 250 nesting pairs, who have produced 335 offspring, at present.[1]

And thus, my career took flight. The article, along with the ruined illustration of the eaglet, was the first of several stories I would write that would appear in *The New York Times*.[2]

Call it serendipity, or call it something much bigger. It was the first in a string of providential encounters that would alter the course of my life. Had the exterminator honored my "Do Not Enter" sign, my life would have been dramatically different. "The Eagle and the Exterminator," as *The New York Times* editor titled my story, swung the door wide open to my future.

Chapter 8

I'd had a fondness for Dr. Michael W. Fox long before I'd ever met him. That's because I would watch with rapt attention each time he was a guest on NBC's *The Tonight Show with Johnny Carson*. He was not only good looking, British, and nearly twenty years my senior, but he was a veterinarian and ethologist—someone who focuses on the behavior of animals in their natural environments—who visited the show repeatedly to teach viewers about the habits of wolves.

So, when I read in the local newspaper that Dr. Fox was coming to a venue a mere twenty miles from my house to give a presentation about animal behavior, wild horses couldn't have kept me away. By this time, he was a vice president at the Washington, DC-based Humane Society of the United States (HSUS), one of the organizations I had been lobbying for a job.

Dr. Fox, author of many books on animal issues, lectured about livestock sentience—the inner lives of cows, calves, pigs, and chickens—and the abuses such animals face on "factory farms." So fascinated was I with his presentation that afterwards, I summoned my courage and waited in the snaking line to speak with him. I then gifted him with a print of an immature barn owl that I had rendered and brought with me. In the ensuing months, Michael and I would become fast friends.

On several subsequent trips to Washington, DC, I visited the Foxes, spending time with Michael, his wife, and their giant but gentle wolf, Tiny. Captive born and raised from a few days of age by Michael, Tiny had been part of the veterinarian's wolf behavioral studies when he had previously worked as a university professor. Michael had commissioned me to draw a portrait of Tiny. Each time I would visit the Foxes—after I sketched and shot reference photos for the portrait—Michael would play his North American

Indigenous flute, and we would all howl in harmony with the magnificent wolf.

I was pleased with the portrait I rendered—Tiny's eyes sparkled, his black nose beaded, and his pink tongue hidden discreetly behind a toothy canine smile. The illustration, coupled with a *New York Times* exposé I wrote on the cruelties of veal calf production,[1] for which I interviewed Michael, would launch a forty-year friendship that would withstand the ravages of time.

Chapter 9

Christine Stevens, widely regarded as the "mother of the animal protection movement," was the founder and president of the Washington, DC-based Animal Welfare Institute (AWI). She had singlehandedly been tackling animal issues since the 1940s, long before I was born. She testified before Congress frequently and had helped push through landmark federal legislation protecting laboratory and slaughter-bound animals. A fierce opponent of commercial whaling and the use of steel-jaw leghold traps for the capture of furbearing animals, she was also one of Washington's elite, an elegant socialite who rubbed elbows with—and received favors from—US presidents, diplomats, and politicians alike. Her husband, Roger, had been a Broadway producer and was the founder of the John F. Kennedy Center for the Performing Arts. Christine was tall, lean, and graceful, and wore her grayish-white hair elegantly pulled back. She had been nicknamed the "duchess of the defenseless."

Mrs. Stevens had been impressed with the *New York Times* articles I had mailed her, and when I traveled again to Washington, DC, she hired me as staff writer on the spot. I was to draft stories about pressing animal welfare issues and get them published in newspapers and magazines with nationwide readership.

The Stevens's gracious old mansion spanned one full block in Washington's tony Georgetown neighborhood; there was a driver to take Mrs. Stevens to Capitol Hill, a personal assistant to manage her social calendar, and a cook to prepare and serve us lunch daily in the mansion's formal dining room. But, early each morning and after lunch, staff filed down the narrow concrete staircase that led to a dank filing cabinet–filled basement; *that* was the nerve center of the Animal Welfare Institute.

My first project for Mrs. Stevens — a feature for *The New York Times* exposing the use of cruel steel-jaw leghold traps by New Jersey trappers[1] — was an enormous success. Published the day before the New Jersey State Senate was to vote on an anti-trapping bill, and distributed to every member of the Senate, the story helped prompt the measure's passage the next day. The controversial bill had been hotly debated in the legislature for the previous eighteen years.

At AWI, I was sort of a jack of all trades. When not writing query letters and articles about animal issues, I edited and illustrated AWI publications and lobbied congressional offices on key animal protection legislation. One field investigation I conducted in Minnesota, which revealed that the prestigious Mayo Clinic was using "random source dogs"—a.k.a. stolen pets—in its laboratory research,[2] gave me a small taste of an investigator's life. Still, the media was not interested in exposing the scandalous story.

In 1951, Dr. Albert Schweitzer had granted permission to the Animal Welfare Institute to strike a medal in his honor, and in 1953, he was the medal's first recipient. The Animal Welfare Institute has, for decades, awarded the Albert Schweitzer Medal to what it calls "shining stars" of the animal protection movement as "a symbol of achievement in the advancement of animal welfare." Over the years, the likes of environmentalist Rachel Carson, ethologist Dr. Jane Goodall, Senator Hubert H. Humphrey, Senator Robert Dole, and US Supreme Court Justice Abe Fortas have been awarded the medal.

Months into my employ at AWI, attending one of the elaborate awards ceremonies, held in a Senate office building of the US Capitol complex, I felt like I had arrived. And indeed, in the world of animal protection, I had. The lofty ceilings and long glistening hallways of the congressional building, the grandeur of the wood paneled hearing room with its ornate molding, it was all very overwhelming to me. I was twenty-eight years old, I had hit the big time, and I was about to tender my resignation.

A World Made Up of Dots 25

Animal protection issues hadn't yet hit mainstream media, and, short of my successes with *The New York Times* and some regional newspapers, my efforts to generate national news coverage seemed difficult, if not in vain. I'd queried publications across the country, pitching stories about wholesale animal cruelty, to no avail. My inability to do what I had come to Washington to do was sapping my already shaky confidence by the day.

Mrs. Stevens was an erudite and accomplished woman, but there was also something about her that reminded me of my hypercritical, authoritarian father. In short, I was a self-conscious jellyfish in her presence. So, after less than a year on the job, feeling ashamed that I had been unable to score any national news stories, I marshalled my confidence, climbed the concrete staircase from the basement to her office on the mansion's main level, and informed Mrs. Stevens that I could no longer work for her; that I had to resign. I would continue trying to get stories placed in national publications on behalf of the organization, but she no longer had to pay me.

Mrs. Stevens accepted my terms.

I thought I was watching my nascent career go up in smoke.

Chapter 10

While working for the Animal Welfare Institute, I had rented a dingy little bedroom in a house at the corner of 34th and Garfield Streets, my temporary home in northwest Washington, DC. The room was furnished with a bed, dresser, table, and chair, and I'd brought my tiny black and white TV with me from home. Five housemates shared the old brick mansion. It was across the street from the Belgian Embassy and a block away from the Naval Observatory—the residence of the US vice president.

Now, assigned to write the annual Christmas appeal letter for the Humane Society of the United States—the nation's largest animal protection organization*—I sat at the little wooden table in my bedroom and jotted down ideas. I was one of two candidates up for the position of staff writer/editor at the organization; I had been asked to write the Christmas fundraiser as part of the job interview process.

I felt certain I had blown the formal interview; I had been nervous and timid throughout. But the words in my Christmas letter flowed straight from my heart; I simply reminded readers that the organization was the only voice that millions of farmed, laboratory, wild, and companion animals would ever have. My work and apparently a good word from my friend Dr. Michael Fox, HSUS vice president for farm animals, landed me the job. My starting salary was $18,000 a year.

Over the next four years—from 1983 until 1987—I churned out hundreds of articles and edited scores of publications. I became intimately familiar with issues confronting animals—from deer hunting on national

---

* In 2025, the Humane Society of the United States would change its name to Humane World for Animals.

wildlife "refuges" to the euthanasia of millions of dogs and cats due to pet overpopulation; from caustic cosmetic testing on laboratory mice to the confinement of captive wildlife in rundown roadside zoos; from abuses to puppies in pet shops to the housing of breeding pigs in cages so cramped they could never turn around—I learned about the many assaults against animals. I literally worked day and night producing compelling stories that reached millions of members. For now, *I* was the voice of the voiceless.

But here's my confession: The main, underlying reason I had worked as a freelance illustrator and writer before going to Washington, DC was because I had long been reluctant to land a "real" job. That was because I did not know when my visual processing problem would flare up. I lived in a state of perpetual fear that, as had been the case years earlier in my high school's gymnasium, and ten thousand times since, I would not be able to process visual input. Depending on my physical environment, I would often become spatially disoriented, as if I were looking into a carnival funhouse mirror or living in a dream.

As mentioned, my visual overload happened when I would take quiet walks in the woods. It had occurred when I'd worked a Christmastime job at Macy's in a suburban New Jersey mall. Some days, I couldn't make sense of my surroundings in the plus-size women's, handbags, or housewares departments where I was stationed. Working the cash register or returning garments from the dressing rooms to the sales racks, my brain was scrambled.

And, most dangerous of all, it happened often when I was driving. With my depth perception impaired, I often couldn't interpret the distance between my vehicle and others, and was overwhelmed as cars and semis whizzed by.

Since the EEG years earlier had shown no irregularities, over time, I blamed myself for my "dyslexia of the world." My mantra, which I would unconsciously repeat whenever my mind was muddled, became, "Why am I doing this to myself?" Visual confusion had become my big, dark secret.

Yet, I somehow managed to hold it together for those four nerve-wracking years that I worked as writer and editor of the HSUS's activist newspaper as well as the organization's quarterly appeal. In each fundraiser, I described a particularly horrific animal issue, with photos and all, followed up by actions members could take to help turn the tide. I took my responsibility as the voice of the voiceless very seriously, and I generated a first-rate product.

Despite my disability, simply writing about animal abuse didn't satisfy me. I longed to get out into the "field," document atrocities like those I had been writing about, and expose them for the world to see. During the last two years of my writing career, I repeatedly asked for a lateral transfer to the HSUS investigations department, but my requests were perfunctorily denied. I watched as investigators from outside the organization came and went. I had been pigeonholed in a job I did well, and management was not going to release me. Finally, I threatened to quit.

That did the trick.

Chapter 11

There were only two national investigators at the Humane Society of the United States: Bob Baker—a former racehorse owner who had exposed the cruel practice of drugging racehorses on the CBS newsmagazine *60 Minutes* and who had been profiled in *The Wall Street Journal* [1]—and me. I was now the only female national investigator working for the largest animal protection organization in the country. I jumped in with both feet.

I traveled the country gathering evidence of abuse at commercial dog breeding establishments (puppy mills), cockfights, factory farms, and ritual animal sacrifices, to name a few. In northern Florida, using the cover of animal illustrator, I insinuated myself into the lives of the country's most successful greyhound owners at one of the nation's busiest training tracks. (A training track is where greyhounds practice racing.) While I'd all but abandoned my drawing career, it came in handy now.

After a few months working to gain the participants' trust, I was able to photograph them hanging "live lures"—live struggling rabbits—upside down from the "whirligig," the mechanical arm that circumnavigates the track. In Florida, it's a felony offense to release greyhounds to chase, and ultimately catch and "savage," the poor bunnies. With the help of law enforcement authorities, we conducted a raid—the first such raid in the country. Twelve participants were prosecuted and/or had their racing licenses suspended.

When not in Florida, I spent weekends driving to livestock auctions in the heart of Virginia's "horse country," where everything from healthy, young Thoroughbreds to broken-down old ponies were sold to the highest bidder: almost always the slaughterhouse "kill buyer." Considered nothing more than a financial burden, unwanted horses were simply hauled off to auction barns where their owners were rewarded with a slaughterhouse check. Thousands of horses were being slaughtered annually in the United States for human consumption; horsemeat burgers and chops were, and are today, a delicacy in Belgium, France, and Japan.

With my visual processing problem, the hour-and-a-half drive from the apartment I now rented in suburban Maryland to Virginia's horse country was stressful. Heat, humidity, and allergies seemed to exacerbate my confusion, and I often found myself pulling off busy Interstate 66 simply to collect myself.

Week after week, at the livestock markets, I shot photos of dead horses, horses with broken noses and legs, burns, infected eyes, gashes, severe malnutrition, pneumonia, and "founder" (inflammation in the foot) so excruciating they could barely walk.

Emaciated, one bay Thoroughbred mare I photographed in a stall in the darkest recesses of the auction barn was too weak to stand and was lying on the manure-packed floor—her legs tucked under her, her hooves overgrown and curled. She was alert.

I climbed up the wood planking at the rear of her stall and photographed her from behind. Barely able to hold her head up, the horse twisted her neck to look back at me, her nose just grazing the unbedded stall floor. Her wide emotive brown eyes gazed at the camera. Sun filtered in through a small window and silhouetted her protruding spine and hip bones and the contours of each rib—a picture worth a thousand words.

Next, I shimmied down the wood planking, gathered up some hay, and knelt directly beside her head. I offered her the fodder, and, after she ate a few handfuls, I gently cradled her head, positioning both arms around her neck, essentially hugging her. I wanted to express a modicum of compassion—to let her know that not all humans were evil. To my astonishment, she completely relaxed her neck muscles and allowed the weight of her heavy head to melt into my arms. Betrayed and nearly starved to death by her human caretaker, she somehow trusted me. Her abject vulnerability touched my heart deeply.

A World Made Up of Dots

An hour later she was sold to the kill buyer for seven dollars—the highest bid. I made sure a veterinarian administered pain medication to her before she was sent on her last journey—to the slaughterhouse.

The day I'd encountered the bay mare at the Front Royal Livestock Exchange, I had enlisted the help of Virginia equine activist Pat Rogers. Pat, then in her fifties, had rescued horses her entire adult life and wanted to establish a sanctuary for abused equines in Virginia. But she had no money, no land, and no stable.

Using the Thoroughbred horse registry, Pat subsequently researched the starving bay mare's identification number that had been tattooed inside her upper lip. We learned that she had been a five-year-old ex-race horse named "Bitsy."

Knowing of its large readership, I persuaded the *National Enquirer* to run a story on horse auctions[2]—an article that included Bitsy's photo and generated roughly forty thousand responses from readers wanting to support our efforts to increase state regulation of auctions. Over the months, I continued to document the deplorable conditions of horses who passed through Virginia's livestock markets, gathering evidence, and ultimately convincing authorities to raid and seize horses from one of the auctions.

Although Bitsy had long been butchered, her life would continue to have an impact. As providence would have it, on Valentine's Day, a small Virginia newspaper ran a story profiling unique local sweethearts. As part of the article, the reporters featured Pat Rogers's love affair with horses, described her desire to start a sanctuary, and ran my photo of Bitsy.

The picture of wide-eyed Bitsy shocked hunt-country readers, who immediately rallied on Pat's behalf. Pat was inundated with offers of support from horse owners, farriers, veterinarians, carpenters, and feed store operators. A landowner offered up a sixty-acre farm, and Equine Rescue League (ERL)—the first sanctuary in Northern Virginia specifically for the rescue of abused horses—was born. Over one thousand visitors attended ERL's grand opening celebration. Within the first six months of operation, sixty-three debilitated horses were given refuge at ERL, and the sanctuary has gone on to rescue thousands more.

Thanks to Pat Rogers and Bitsy, in Virginia's horse country, there is now a sanctuary for abused equines. Today, a framed photograph of Bitsy hangs prominently in the main office at Equine Rescue League's Promise Kept Farm. It is a constant reminder of, and a testament to, the fact that Bitsy—and the hundreds of Bitsys we could not rescue—did not die in vain.

Part Two

A Fortress Around My Heart

Chapter 12

After receiving the letter from slaughterhouse whistleblower Timothy Walker, I booked the next flight to southwest Florida, where I would meet the informant for the first time. As we sat at a corner table in a small, brightly lit seafood restaurant—he with a sandwich, me, a salad—Tim explained to me what was going on.

I learned that Walker was a USDA brucellosis tester at Kaplan Industries, the biggest cattle slaughterhouse in Florida. Stationed on a catwalk in the "blood pit," he said, he routinely encountered live cows having their heads skinned while they were still fully conscious. As a result, animals hanging upside down from the "bleed rail" would kick and struggle wildly. Occasionally, they would free themselves, crashing headfirst to the floor fifteen feet below. While Tim was worried about his safety and that of his coworkers, his greatest concern was for the poor cows.

Having written letters about the violations to all his USDA supervisors, to members of Congress, and to the Veteran's Administration (he was a former Navy sailor), and having received no response, Tim decided to bypass the federal government altogether and seek help from outside. Concerned and frustrated, he reached out to several animal protection organizations across the United States. "I have contacted a number of federal agencies but have been told there is nothing they can do," his letter said. "They also told me that the problems I described exist all over the country, that they are just a little worse at Kaplan's." Mine was the only response Walker received.

The federal Humane Methods of Slaughter Act (HMSA), enacted in 1958, requires that animals in slaughterhouses be humanely handled and that they be rendered unconscious prior to being shackled, hoisted up on the rail, and butchered. Cattle are rendered insensible by a "stun operator" or "knocker" who uses a "captive bolt" gun to deliver a blow to the cow's head. A captive bolt gun, powered by compressed air or a blank cartridge, drives a retractable steel bolt into an animal's head. Regulations require that the animal be rendered unconscious with a *single application* of the captive bolt gun.

USDA meat inspectors and veterinarians stationed in slaughterhouses are the officials charged with enforcing the HMSA. They are required to stop the slaughter line—halt production—when they observe humane violations. Unfortunately, examining livestock before slaughter (antemortem inspection) and animals' heads, viscera, and carcasses after slaughter (postmortem inspection) was—and continues to be—meat inspectors' number one job. Because inspectors didn't venture into the "blood pit" where animals are slaughtered, enforcing the Humane Methods of Slaughter Act was not even a blip on their radar screen.

"Last Saturday," Walker told me, "the line was smoking. There were more live cows coming through than I've ever seen before. The skinners were cussing. We were cussing. The whole line was going crazy. Just about every cow that come down the line—at least a hundred of them—was alive that afternoon."

Tim blamed the problem on the dilapidated plant, poorly maintained stunning equipment, and the fact that plant supervisors tried to push through too many cows.

I ultimately tracked down and interviewed three USDA brucellosis testers—Tim's coworkers—who had been stationed at the plant. "Tim's out of his element; he's just too sensitive for the job," said one. Another explained that when he had stopped production for conscious cows, the plant owner had threatened his government job. The third said that USDA had seen to it that a small sheet of metal was erected overhead to protect workers. "It could hardly have saved us from kicking or falling cows," she said. Despite being scared that disclosing the truth could cost them their jobs, when push came to shove, all three coworkers bravely came forward and corroborated Tim's claims.

A fourth brucellosis tester—who had been injured dodging a flailing cow at the plant—had agreed earlier to meet with me, but then had abruptly changed his mind. Instead, the blabbermouth went to his supervisors, ratting out Tim for voicing his concerns outside the agency.

Two days later, Tim received a letter from a senior USDA bureaucrat. "I have determined that your overall conduct is nonacceptable and that your continued employment is not in the best interest of Federal Service," the official wrote. USDA's relationship with Kaplan Industries "was almost destroyed by your decision to take your criticism to the public *rather than through the Agency itself.* Your general traits are incompatible with the duties related to your position. It is my decision that to continue your employment would impede the efficiency of government service." And with those words, Timothy Walker, a heroic federal whistleblower, was unceremoniously sacked.

Chapter 13

Because most company workers at Kaplan Industries were of Mexican descent, I headed to a few Spanish-speaking communities about a half-hour south of the plant. At a convenience store that cashed Kaplan paychecks, I was pointed in the direction of a slaughterhouse employee who lived a few blocks away. Sharing a house on a dusty dirt road with nine migrant grapefruit pickers, the Kaplan employee independently confirmed everything that Tim had alleged.

"My job was to wash the heads," he said, in a taped interview. "I could see just about everything from where I worked." That included cows thrashing wildly from the overhead rail, employees cutting the spinal cords in cows' necks to stop the kicking, and a line speed too fast for the men to keep up.

I located another employee who lived in a tidy white trailer on the far side of town. I asked him exactly how he knew the cows were alive. "They're hanging down and still yelling, 'Moo!'" he exclaimed. "They pick up their heads, and their eyes look around. Everybody could tell those cows were alive."

Next, I visited a low-income housing project; there was graffiti on the doorways and shattered glass on the ground. After pounding on the apartment door, with no response, I waited for several hours outside the building. When the worker arrived home, I followed him through the doorway, introducing myself as I went inside.

I had hit pay dirt. I would learn that the man, named Albert, had recently been Kaplan's stun operator—the individual who was supposed to render the animals unconscious. He could best corroborate Walker's claims.

"In the morning, the big holdup was the calves," the worker said. To speed up the stunning process, he explained, employees would put nine calves in the knocking box at one time. "As soon as they start going in, you start shooting, the calves are jumping, they're all piling up on top of each other." Unaware which animals he had effectively knocked, he would neglect to stun the calves on the bottom. "They're hung anyway, and down the line they go, wriggling and yelling."

Albert said it wasn't just calves who were being butchered alive. "It was a serious problem with the cows," he continued, "and the bulls have even harder skulls. A lot I had to hit them three or five times, ten times before they'd go down. There were plenty of times you'd have to make a big hole in their head and still they'd be alive."

According to Albert, the USDA veterinarian in charge of the plant knew full well what was going on; she would stand near the knocker and watch him deliver repeated blows to cows' heads. "I'd be shooting every one five, six times," he said. "She'd yell at me but she would never stop the line. They don't slow that line down for nothing or nobody."

Finally, wanting an airtight case, I located a former Kaplan supervisor who lived a few blocks from the slaughterhouse. A handsome man with curly brown hair, he agreed to talk about the treatment of non-ambulatory cows—animals who couldn't walk or stand. "On bad days you'd have over thirty downers," he explained. "These animals only got food or water if they could drag themselves up to the hay or water troughs." With extremely high fevers, no veterinary care, and unable to stand, he said, these cows were left in the baking sun for days, starving, dehydrated, until they eventually died.

Chapter 14

Back at the office, I was furiously transcribing audiotapes; at the same time, Tim's letter was replaying over and over in my head. "I have contacted a number of federal agencies," he'd written. "They told me that the problems I described *exist all over the country, that they are just a little worse at Kaplan's*." I wondered exactly what that meant—just what were conditions like at thousands of slaughterhouses across the United States?

I was nowhere near finished with Walker's case, and now, thanks to me, Tim was out of a job. Then, two days later, amongst a pile of complaints in my inbox—an Oklahoma teenager went on a strangling spree at a pet store, a Missouri farmer starved one thousand pigs to death, a Texas man videotaped himself having sex with his dog – I stumbled across an article in glossy *The Animals Voice Magazine*. According to the story, a union official at an Iowa slaughterhouse alleged that hogs there were not being properly stunned. As a result, they were being shackled, hoisted up onto the overhead rail kicking and struggling, and not being adequately bled. Consequently, said the official, hogs were being immersed into John Morrell & Company's scalding tank alive. "What the public sees is fancy labels . . . but those of us inside the walls can tell the truth about what the vast majority have never seen—living hell in John Morrell's slaughterhouse," he said. The article was accompanied by a full-page color photo of the "sticker"—the man who cuts the hogs' throats—his shiny white apron streaked with blood.[1]

I caught a flight to Sioux City, Iowa, to meet with the union official. He told me that the sticker who appeared in the photo, a sandy-haired man in his twenties, had since been violently slashed by his own knife. A live hog dangling from the moving rail had kicked the sticker's knife, slicing him

40

A Fortress Around My Heart

diagonally across his face. It had taken four hours of surgery and 125 stitches to sew up the gash. Tired of cutting the throats of live, thrashing hogs, sticker Tommy Vladak had quit his job at the slaughterhouse, packed up his family, and moved ten hours south. I got in my rental car and headed to his mobile home in western Kansas.

Unlike cows, who are stunned by a blow to the head, hogs are either rendered unconscious or killed through the administration of CO_2 gas—which has serious animal welfare implications as hogs often struggle to escape, gasp, shake their heads, and emit high-pitched vocalizations—or the application of electricity. At John Morrell, electrodes were being applied to hogs' heads and backs for a jolt of electricity that was supposed to knock out the animals and cause cardiac arrest. But, according to Vladak, the voltage discharged by Morrell's stunning wand left small bruises on the backs of some hogs. That translated to a cosmetic defect on packages of pork loins in the supermarket meat case. Thus, to prevent "bruised loins," Morrell supervisors resorted to turning the electric current down. While hogs were still subjected to an electrical shock, they were neither rendered unconscious nor killed by the jolt. Dazed, the animals were shackled and hoisted up on the overhead rail, and down the line they went.

"I was kicked, bitten, stabbed in the forearm, had a tooth knocked out, an eardrum punctured, and finally got my face slashed," Vladak shared when I met up with him in my motel room one night. "And that was after I complained about live hogs to almost every level of management, and had shut the chain off a bunch of times trying to deal with the problem." Vladak was sticking about nine hundred hogs an hour—relatively slow by industry standards. "It wouldn't be that hard if they were stunned right," he continued. "But when most of them are conscious, kicking and biting at you, it's like . . ." He tried to think of an analogy. "It's like I could've gone ten rounds with Mike Tyson and whooped his ass.

"It got to the point if I had a live hog come at me and I had time, I'd take a lead pipe and beat it over the head until it was knocked out enough for me to stick it."

After leaving the sticker, hogs traveled up a ramp where they were immersed into a vat of 140-degree water—the scalding tank—to loosen and remove their hair. "By the time they hit the scalding tank, they're still fully conscious and squealing," said Vladak. "Happens all the time."

I met Ed Van Winkle—a former Morrell employee who had worked every kill floor job at ten different plants—for an early breakfast at a coffee shop downtown. "The sticker doesn't have time to go digging around for arteries," he explained. "Bad sticks usually don't have a chance to bleed out.

"These hogs get up to the scalding tank, hit the water and they start screaming and kicking," Van Winkle said, independently corroborating Vladak's claims. "There's a rotating arm that pushes hogs under, no chance for them to get out. I'm not sure if they burn to death before they drown, but it takes them a couple of minutes to stop thrashing."

Van Winkle looked pensive as he thought about what to say next. "Management doesn't care how the hog gets up on that line. Management doesn't care whether the hog is stunned or conscious, or whether the sticker is injured in the process. All Morrell cares about is getting those hogs killed."

With remorse in his eyes, the worker recounted stories of abuses he'd inflicted on his innocent victims. "If you work in that stick pit for any period of time, you develop an attitude that lets you kill things but doesn't let you care. Pigs down on the kill floor have come up and nuzzled me like a puppy. Two minutes later I had to kill them—beat them to death with a pipe. I can't care."

As a union safety representative, Van Winkle had begged and pleaded with Morrell management to take corrective action. He had futilely reached out to the USDA veterinarian in charge of the plant and to state safety officials as well. "I couldn't stand by and watch any longer," he said. "I had to get out." Fed up and disgusted, he finally quit his job. He was back in community college studying to be, of all things, a registered nurse.

A Fortress Around My Heart   43

"Once in a while, when school gets too rough, I go take a tour at Morrell's," he said. "Last time I went down there I saw the same live hogs—nothing's changed. There are a few different faces, but all the expressions are the same."

The employees I'd spoken with had worked the night shift; I needed to investigate what was happening in the light of day. Donny Tice was the day shift sticker, so one evening, I drove my rental car up the hilly streets of Sioux City to his modest home. After answering the door, Tice explained to me that he wasn't a union member; without the protection of the union, he was reluctant to speak out. But with the help of a Michelob and some light conversation, the flood gates burst wide open.

"Down in the blood pit they say that the smell of blood makes you aggressive," he started. "And it does. You get an attitude that if that hog kicks at me, I'm going to get even. You're already going to kill the hogs, but that's not enough. It has to suffer. When you get a live one you think, oh good, I'm going to beat this sucker." For Tice, that meant poking hogs' eyes out, slicing off noses, and making hogs drown in their own blood.

I could hardly believe my ears and the fact that Tice was letting me tape record his confession. I tried to remain unruffled to keep him on his roll.

"One time, there was a live hog in the pit," he recalled. "It hadn't done anything wrong, wasn't even running around the pit. It was just alive. I took a three-foot chunk of pipe, and I literally beat that hog to death. Couldn't have been a two-inch piece of solid bone left in its head. It was like I started hitting the hog and I couldn't stop."

After listening to himself regale me with cruelty, Tice had a change of heart. He declared that after eleven years in the industry, he was getting out of "the pack."

I interviewed other workers who described gratuitous acts of cruelty that they were performing for fun. They delighted in half-stunning hogs to watch them "freak out" and in chasing them into the scalding tank for the sheer amusement of the prank.

"Hogs are stubborn," said one old-timer. "Beating them in the head seems to work about the best. You force a hog down the alley, have another guy standing there with a piece of rebar in his hand—"

"Yeah, it's like playing baseball," replied a coworker.

"Like someone pitching something at you," the old-timer said with a chortle.

The culture of abuse at John Morrell had had profound consequences for workers: the employees I'd interviewed had paid a high price. Several had become alcoholics and drug abusers; some had admitted to slapping their wives around. Employees had described their homicidal fantasies; some had become assailants and been sentenced to serve time in jail.

"After a while, you become desensitized," Donny Tice had confided. "I used to be very sensitive about people's problems—willing to listen. As far as animals go, they're a lower life-form. They're maybe one step above a maggot."

Perhaps Donny Tice and the other workers weren't the only ones who had become desensitized. Maybe I was desensitized, too? Surely, a healthy person documenting such heinous crimes against animals would have felt repulsed, compelled to run from these perpetrators at the first mention of the atrocities they had committed. I was so cut off from my feelings—perhaps a protective mechanism—and so determined to let the world in on the meat industry's dirty secrets, that I could not allow myself to feel revolted, I could not allow myself to feel, period. I approached this assignment like all the other cruelty cases I had investigated: emotionally numb, distanced, and detached.

Chapter 15

I hadn't forgotten about poor Timothy Walker who was still in south Florida, unemployed. Back at my office, I found myself working well after business hours each evening, feverishly transcribing tapes, preparing affidavits, and, in short, trying to put together open-and shut-cases against Kaplan and John Morrell. I felt the weight of the world on me; there wasn't a moment to spare.

My eyes continued to play tricks on me. Whether in my office, on the road, in retail stores, or in my apartment's living room, I often felt confused. Dim lighting overwhelmed my senses and muddled my brain. Then again, so did fluorescent bulbs. (I had early on in my tenure at HSUS replaced the overhead lights in my office with full spectrum illumination; that seemed to calm my nervous system down a bit.)

On any given day—aware that animals were being skinned and boiled alive on my watch—I would work obsessively until late afternoon when I'd take a brief break. From HSUS headquarters, I'd walk across the street to a corner grocery to pick up a quick lunch. Each time I entered the crowded, brightly lit market—its shelves crammed with goods, people milling about, and lines at the registers—I felt like I was back in my high school gymnasium on that damned basketball court. Bombarded with visual input and in a dreamlike state, it was all I could do to make my purchase and get out as fast as I'd arrived. Dazed and confused, I'd exit the store, go back to the office, and work late into the night.

Unaware that there even was a federal Humane Methods of Slaughter Act, union officials at John Morrell had sent a letter about live, struggling hogs to the local animal shelter. The letter was ultimately forwarded to the

USDA. Knowing of this letter's existence, I submitted a federal Freedom of Information Act request to the USDA to obtain the agency's response.

"I've observed slaughter procedures and have seen no problems with sticking hogs at this speed," wrote the USDA veterinarian in charge at John Morrell to his district supervisor. "I will continue to monitor sticking procedures. If problems occur, immediate action will be taken. I do not feel we have a problem at this time."

While I wanted to prepare cases against Kaplan and Morrell, it was inconceivable we would get animal cruelty convictions against what were among the biggest employers—and biggest taxpayers—in their respective towns. What's more, even if we convinced a prosecutor to take the case, the charges could be plea bargained down, dismissed on a technicality, or the defendants could be acquitted by a jury of their "peers." Even more troubling, and further reducing our chances, was the fact that federal law preempts state law, and USDA inspectors were inside the plants, supposedly enforcing federal law. My strategy was to expand the scope of the investigation—document humane violations at more slaughterhouses—and then expose, through the national media, the USDA's role in allowing violations to persist.

Thanks to the blabbermouth who'd ratted out Timothy Walker, USDA officials in Florida were well aware of my investigation. Instead of taking corrective action at Kaplan Industries, USDA supervisors had issued a de facto "gag order" to government workers, threatening employees with the loss of their jobs if they spoke with me. Tim Walker was living proof they meant business. In Iowa, on the other hand, with the exception of the incompetent USDA veterinarian who had "observed no problems" and took no action, the USDA knew nothing about the abuses being perpetrated at John Morrell.

I couldn't bear the thought of animals being scalded alive while I was busy executing my strategic plan. Morrell's humane slaughter consultant—an animal scientist who the company paid to periodically review slaughter practices—was a colleague of mine. The least I could do without jeopardizing my case was to alert her to the violations at the plant. (According to my sources, when she'd inspected the facility in the past, supervisors had collected lead pipes and turned the stunning current up. They had put on a convincing show for her.)

She was reluctant to take me at my word, so I put her in touch with the employees themselves. Her subsequent actions, however, did little to correct the problem. On the contrary, to cover their bases, Morrell supervisors made employees sign "statements of humaneness," but they didn't stop overseeing animal abuse and turning the stunner current down.

Chapter 16

A few weeks later, I received a tip from two Illinois horse enthusiasts who'd heard from their friend—a slaughterhouse worker—about violations at his plant. They would put me in touch with an unlikely informant. I'd photographed horses being killed before—their shoed hooves tossed in haphazard piles on the slaughterhouse floor—but nothing could've prepared me for what this witness would have to say.

Steve Parrish, a thirty-something African American man, ran with a rough crowd from the South Side of Chicago. A drug conviction had recently landed him in a medium security prison about two hours west of the Windy City.

I proceeded through prison security, where I was searched from head to toe. Next, I was ushered through a series of sliding steel doors into a large cinder block room with tables and chairs fixed in place. A uniformed guard was stationed in a booth where he monitored everyone's moves. The half-hour prisoner count buzzed twice before Steve Parrish finally entered the room. A prison guard directed him over to me.

Over the last few weeks, Parrish and I had spoken on the phone a number of times, he calling from prison, me accepting the charges. Thus, when we met, it felt like we were old friends. After hugging and exchanging pleasantries, we got down to business.

Before he was incarcerated, Parrish had worked at an Illinois horse slaughterhouse, at the time, the only horse packing plant in the Midwest. From our previous conversations, I knew that the operation, which butchered horses for human consumption overseas, was rife with violations. What I didn't know was that Parrish's coworkers had been busy stealing pet horses

A Fortress Around My Heart

from small area farms, animals that they would transport to the plant, and furtively slaughter under cover of night.

"The boss needed more meat to ship to Belgium," Parrish said. "We'd stay over after the USDA doc left, or go back in the middle of the night." For participating in this criminal activity, Parrish received a bonus of twenty dollars in his paycheck for each horse he butchered. "We'd kill anything from thirty to forty horses at night."

I asked Parrish about the treatment of downed horses in the light of day. "If we kick a horse and he's '2D' [downed or disabled] and we can't move him, I'd split his throat in the pens and let him bleed, cut his nerves off at the back of the neck. Because you could work with him better when he's dead."

If horses collapsed in alleyways, I would learn, workers would beat them with pipes or pieces of wood, kick them, or stab them with knives. If that didn't do the trick, they would wrap a cable around the animals' necks and drag them with a hoist, choking them. After all, a downed horse in the alleyway spelled slowed production, and, in the slaughterhouse biz, time is money.

"You've got to have something for whatever situation you're in," Parrish explained. "You can't spend fifteen or twenty minutes on one horse. You have to do whatever you can to get him in that box to get him skinned—fast. You can't let one horse stop you from making money."

While the stun operator was supposed to render each horse unconscious with a single blow square on the animal's forehead, the knocker often delivered repeated shots. "I've seen them shoot them five times, hit them all in the eye. Hit them in the neck. I've seen horses get shot wrong and get right back up and walk around the kill floor, kind of dazed. And they run up on them and just hit them with the knife in the neck, anywhere, and just let them suffer, walk around bleeding."

Compounding the problem at this horse plant was the fact that the sticker and the head skinner were one and the same person. (After sticking, animals are supposed to be given several minutes to bleed out before being butchered.) "You move so fast you don't have time to wait till a horse bleed out," said Parrish. "You skin him as he bleeds."

Parrish then related details from his previous jobs working at hog and cattle slaughterhouses, confirming everything I'd already heard. "I actually seen a hog that wasn't stuck right jump out of the scald tank with the steam still smoking off his body. He jumped out and was hollering. Not sticking them right and dropping them in the tank alive, that happens at a lot of slaughterhouses.

"I've drug cows till their bones start breaking, while they were still alive. Bringing them around the corner and they get stuck up in the doorway, just pull till their hide be ripped, till their blood just drip on the steel and concrete. Breaking their legs pulling them in. And the cow be crying with its tongue stuck out. They pull him till his neck just pop."

I had accomplished my goal. I told the prisoner it was time for me to go. We both stood up, hugged one more time, and out the sliding steel doors I went.

Back at my Maryland apartment, the visual processing problem I experienced was affected by lighting levels, weather, and motion. In the city, office buildings, traffic, and general hustle bustle conspired to compete for my attention. The drive into work, down Connecticut Avenue to HSUS headquarters, was precarious, at best. When I traveled on the DC beltway, it was almost suicide. I refused to capitulate to my problem, and I kept right on going, blaming myself in the process. "Why am I doing this to myself?" was my refrain.

It seemed to me that with each round of violations I documented, my eye problem was getting worse. Was this psychosomatic? Was there something I didn't want to "see"?

I had visited ophthalmologists, neurologists, and allergists, to name a few, and now I didn't know where to turn. So, one lunchtime, I walked the busy DC sidewalks to a suite of offices—a psychiatric practice—near the city's Dupont Circle hub.

It wasn't the first time nor would it be the last that I would visit a psychiatrist's office. As a child in the 1960s, I had seen a psychiatrist, my parents trying to understand what afflicted me. Obsessive compulsive disorder hadn't become a household term yet. In fact, OCD wouldn't even be classified as an anxiety disorder for another twenty years. Nobody knew why I had those strange compulsions—not my parents, not the psychiatrist, and least of all, not me.

In 1990s Washington, DC, the doctor prescribed a cocktail of anti-anxiety drugs for my visual processing problem. Pharmaceutical commercials hadn't yet overtaken the airwaves, so the stigma of taking Buspar, Tofranil, and Xanax—used for the treatment of generalized anxiety—was my personal shame. I felt so alone—so uniquely different from my coworkers. To my knowledge, none of them had been prescribed psychotropic drugs. But, more to the point, I felt helpless and scared; how was I going to function with spatial disorientation? How was I going to continue to do my job? I tried the drug cocktail for six months. In the end, it did nothing to improve my perceptual problem.

I continued to crisscross the country following many leads, and, in some cases, just randomly selecting slaughterhouses to ascertain what was going on. In South Dakota, a sticker at a large beef kill complained of fully conscious cattle reaching his station.

"The way I look at it," said the sticker, "out of the 1,228 beef I stuck today it would have been okay if a few were still alive. But it's all day. Constantly, all day, I get live cattle."

"There's only one guy to stick all three thousand beef we do all day," said a worker at a Nebraska plant. "I've seen beef still alive at the 'flankers,' more often at the 'ears and horns.' I've seen them over where they take the hide off with the down puller"—that's a machine that peels back the hide from the animal's torso—"I've heard them moo when people with air knives were trying to take the hide off. I think it's cruel for the animal to be dying little by little while everybody's doing their various jobs on it."

Nor were the violations I documented limited to slaughter. I learned of humane handling abuses too numerous to count. Workers described jabbing electric prods in animals' anuses, ears, eyes, and mouths. Disabled livestock were dragged with Bobcat tractors and chains. A cow trapped in a collapsed truck had her leg removed with a saw. A steer caught in an alleyway had his leg blow torched off. A bull wedged in a gate had his head cut off while alive. Young pigs bound for rendering were, in the words of a witness, "clubbed to death like baby seals."

And then there were problems with transportation, where hogs shipped in subzero temperatures would arrive at plants frozen solid. "I've seen a lot of 'frozens,'" said one yard worker. "I've seen as many as sixty dead ones off a truck."

"Hogs freeze to that steel railing," said another. "They're still alive, and they'll hook a cable on it and pull it out, maybe pull a leg off."

One of the workers shot video of an employee chainsawing frozen, rock-solid hogs into pieces to deposit into the "rendering hole." (Rendered hogs are used in the production of everything from livestock feed and lubricants to linoleum and lipstick; pork industry officials often brag that they use every part of the pig "but the squeal.") The video also depicted mountains of dead, frozen hogs that were awaiting chainsawing.

"When they come off the truck, they're solid as a block of ice," said a worker at that plant. "Sometimes they'd be so froze that you'd have to take a hot water hose to thaw them apart." The employee described finding live frozen hogs in the piles of dead. "I took my ax chopper and chopped them to death. Hit them in the head. I told my supervisor that they'd been frozen alive and that I'd killed them. He said, 'Oh, that's fine.'"

Looking back, I wish I could've cried—or even raged—about the animal victims as I recorded these brutal accounts, these litanies of horror. But I couldn't. My feelings were frozen, buried deep inside me. I knew in my head that the crimes I was documenting were horrific, but I couldn't make the leap from my head to my heart. Instead, I just did the next right thing, putting one foot in front of the other, interviewing, listening, taping, transcribing, and ultimately turning these shameful admissions, these confessions of sins, into declarations and affidavits to be signed by the perpetrators themselves.

It's not surprising then that, at night, I would dream about farm animal abuse. In one all-too-vivid dream, I was a shackled hog on a bloody kill floor, screaming loudly, but no one could hear my cries over the din of the disassembly line. Just as the sticker was about to plunge his knife into my throat, I abruptly awoke, gasping for air.

Thus, it follows that when not on the road investigating, or in my office transcribing, I invariably found myself waiting patiently in doctors' offices, first it was for shortness of breath; later, it was a persistent lump in my throat; and finally, I was literally doubled over with abdominal pain. It always seemed to be something. What I didn't realize at the time was that I was stuffing the atrocities down my throat, and they had to come out some way.

Chapter 17

In addition to transcribing tapes and preparing affidavits, I was busy executing my strategic plan: to expose slaughterhouse abuses across the country and reveal USDA's role in allowing them to persist. I labored for weeks—extracting salient quotes from worker interviews and preparing a succinct summary of violations—all in the hopes of hooking the press. My first stop: the CBS news magazine *60 Minutes*.

After much poking and prodding, a *60 Minutes* producer became tepidly interested in the story. Against his executive producer's wishes who thought the issue "too disgusting," the producer followed me out to South Dakota; his correspondent was scheduled to fly in a few days later to interview ten employees from two plants. They had courageously agreed to go on camera. I was hopeful that the violations would finally be exposed nationally and the animals' suffering would at long last end.

But when the producer got wind of a contract dispute between the union and plant management over wages, he became suspicious of the workers' claims. Paranoid about a possible lawsuit against CBS, and despite my tearful appeals, he killed the story on the spot. He canceled the correspondent's inbound trip and booked the next available flight out of town.

Deserted by the one person who I thought could help end the abuses, I felt momentarily inconsolable, disheartened beyond words. I believed I had failed both the animals and the slaughterhouse workers who were counting on me.

Over the course of the next several months, I FedExed mountains of documentation first to a senior producer at ABC's *20/20* and then to two producers at that network's *Primetime Live*. All three expressed strong interest in airing the story. Unfortunately, when push came to shove, they each independently concluded that the subject matter was too graphic and decided to pull the plug. The networks routinely featured human victims of stabbings, shootings, and starvation on the news, yet they didn't have the guts to cover what their viewers were unwittingly subsidizing? How was I going to stop the abuse, I wondered, if I couldn't get anyone to expose it?

I felt like I was back where I had started.

By now, I had made inroads with the National Joint Council of Food Inspection Locals (NJC), the federal union representing the nation's six thousand USDA meat inspectors. Talking with the chairman of that union, I was able to establish that USDA inspectors—the very individuals charged with enforcing the Humane Methods of Slaughter Act—were being prevented from doing that job.

"The way the plants are physically laid out," the chairman explained to me in a videotaped interview, "meat inspection is way down the line. A lot of times inspectors can't see the slaughter area from their stations," he said. "It's virtually impossible for them to monitor the slaughter area when they're trying to detect diseases and abnormalities in carcasses that are whizzing by."

I asked him how often inspectors visited the slaughter area.

"And leave their stations? If an inspector did that, he'd be subject to disciplinary action for abandoning his inspection duties. Inspectors are tied to the line."

Next, I inquired about the protocol for checking on humane slaughter compliance.

"There isn't one," he answered.

"Hold on," I said, astonished. "You're telling me that inspectors have the authority to stop the line when they see humane violations, but basically, they're never allowed to see them?"

"That's right. Very seldom do inspectors ever go into that area and actually enforce humane handling and slaughter. They can't. *They're not allowed to*. The Humane Methods of Slaughter Act is a regulation on paper only," he explained. "It is not being enforced."

Bingo. I had gotten it straight from the horse's mouth. The Humane Methods of Slaughter Act had been passed in 1958. Regulations had been promulgated twenty years later, granting federal meat inspectors the authority to enforce that law. Had it all been a sham, a farce, a big charade? Inspectors couldn't stop the line when they witnessed animal cruelty because they were never permitted to see what was going on? It all added up to me now. The chairman, I thought, had been remarkably forthcoming. It had been an astounding admission.

This abandonment of their humane responsibilities was confirmed by dozens of inspectors who I subsequently interviewed. They confided in me that if, by some quirk of fate, they happened to observe humane violations and stop the line, they would be subject to disciplinary action by their USDA supervisors or fired for impeding plant production. Talk about adding insult to injury.

Reeling from—and validated by—these revelations, I felt it was time to go back to the press.

Chapter 18

Things were a-changing at HSUS. The organization's president fell hook, line, and sinker for a fellow named David Wills and before I knew what was happening, Wills had been appointed my immediate boss. It was common knowledge among my coworkers that, in his previous positions as executive director of the Michigan Humane Society and president of the Nashua, New Hampshire, Humane Society, Wills had left amid allegations of misuse of funds. A con artist who had faked his resume and altered his academic record to mask time spent in jail for burglary was now vice president of investigations for HSUS.[1]

Wills informed me that I was no longer permitted to speak with the media about my slaughterhouse investigation. I wondered, if I can't talk to the press, what the heck am I supposed to do with this information? Suddenly, it seemed that not only was I battling the abusers, but I was fighting my own supervisor—the very person who was supposed to be protecting the animals!

Ignoring his directive, in a last-ditch effort to publicize my slaughterhouse findings, I sent the videotaped interview I'd conducted with the chairman of the meat inspectors' union to the networks and re-pitched the story again. After all, here was the individual representing all six thousand meat inspectors saying that his members were being prevented by their supervisors from carrying out their congressional mandate. When it came to humane slaughter enforcement, inspectors' hands were effectively tied.

Unmoved, with their heels dug in, all four network producers were concerned that the story was too upsetting for public consumption. After all, viewers might have just eaten a sirloin steak or pork chop dinner, and we wouldn't want them changing channels.

I'd heard it all before.

Meanwhile, down in Florida, Timothy Walker had been out of a job for the better part of a year. Since I was confident that Walker's termination had been in clear violation of the federal Whistleblower Protection Act, with help from a Washington, DC, whistleblower law firm, we filed a complaint with the U.S. Office of Special Counsel (OSC) on Tim's behalf. (The OSC is a federal agency that investigates reprisals against whistleblowers.) We listed violations of fourteen federal humane and safety regulations at Kaplan Industries, ranging from improper stunning of cattle to animals falling from the rail threatening workers below.

If the OSC ruled that there was a "substantial likelihood" that Walker had been illegally fired—a decision it rarely issues—that agency would require USDA officials to conduct a thorough investigation at the packing plant and issue a report. To our amazement, the OSC ruled in Walker's favor, triggering a review by the USDA. Finally, a piece of good news! I called Tim with the update; we shared a triumphant moment over the phone.

Our celebration was short-lived. Days after the USDA probe was conducted at the slaughterhouse and before its findings were issued in a report, Kaplan Industries—one of the biggest beef packers in the southeastern United States, which, according to *The Tampa Tribune*, planned to expand operations—suddenly and inexplicably went out of business. Shuttered its facility. Closed up shop.

So, why had Kaplan abruptly shut its doors? I did some digging. The former president of the National Cattlemen's Association was a celebrated beef industry spokesperson. Now, as USDA's assistant secretary for marketing and inspection services, she was the nation's top meat inspector, the senior-most official responsible for enforcement of the Humane Methods of Slaughter Act. She was also a fifth-generation Florida cattle rancher whose animals apparently had been sold through local auction to where else? Kaplan Industries.

What a scandal that would have been. If word had leaked that the assistant secretary's cattle were having their heads skinned while still alive, in a plant under her authority, it could have been a devastating blow to the beef industry and USDA.

Two months later, with the plant no longer operating, USDA delivered its final report. In his written findings, the US Secretary of Agriculture determined that Walker's charges were unfounded because, he explained, the stunning, shackling, and sticking areas were all off limits to federal inspectors; they were *not stations where USDA personnel performed their tasks.*

Tim and I were astounded by this disclosure; we knew we had caught the secretary in our trap. After all, if USDA inspectors weren't allowed into those areas of the plants, the secretary left us wondering just how they could enforce the Humane Methods of Slaughter Act?

"Based upon the findings of the inquiry," the secretary summarized in his glowing report, a cover-up of unprecedented proportions, "it is our conclusion that USDA officials assigned to the establishment have enforced the Humane Methods of Slaughter Act."

The secretary's lies left us wondering just how far USDA would go to protect its meat industry cronies. After all, this wasn't some low-level bureaucrat touting the party line. This was the highest-ranking agriculture official in the country, a member of President George H. W. Bush's cabinet, initiating a cover up!

Walker testified before Congress on the issue, and we prepared a comprehensive rebuttal to the Secretary, excerpting the extensive interviews I had conducted with the USDA and Kaplan personnel, and using the secretary's own words against him. In the end, Walker won his job back, with an impressive settlement package designed to keep us out of court. But Walker and I were hardly ecstatic; we were no closer to exposing slaughterhouse atrocities that had occurred at Kaplan's or those that were happening across the United States.

Chapter 19

One Tuesday afternoon, HSUS executives held a meeting at headquarters to discuss my slaughterhouse case. I was not invited, nor was I permitted to attend. Because anger at anyone other than myself didn't come naturally to me, I was more speechless than anything else.

During the course of the meeting, David Wills bragged to his supervisors that he knew of a Detroit slaughterhouse where hogs weren't being properly stunned. He said the animals there were doubling up at the abdomen—essentially struggling to right themselves—while hanging from the rail. He knew about the violations because, having previously worked for Michigan Humane Society, he had an informant at the plant.

When I learned about his assertions from a coworker who had attended the meeting, I made a beeline for my new boss.

"Do you know if it's happening now?" I politely inquired. (Wills and I weren't on the best of terms.)

"I assume that it is," he responded, rocking back in his chair behind his oversized desk.

"If you have your informant's phone number, I'd be glad to give him a call."

Wills, protective of his source, declined my offer, but agreed to phone him on my behalf. He reported back to me after making the call.

"He says it's definitely still a problem," Wills assured me. "Hogs on the chain—they're trying to right themselves."

I was scheduled to travel to Illinois to interview another employee at the horse slaughterhouse where Steve Parrish had worked, and I had leads on workers at two Michigan plants. The timing couldn't have been better. I would add Wills's Detroit slaughterhouse to my list.

A Fortress Around My Heart   61

I asked my supervisor to arrange a meeting between me and his source. He agreed to phone his informant a second time, and, after repeated reminders, he said he'd made the call. But the informant refused to meet with me. He was afraid of losing his job. Disappointed but not discouraged, I decided to visit the plant anyway to see what I could uncover.

With the exception of the horse auctions I'd attended with Pat Rogers, founder of Virginia's Equine Rescue League, I'd always worked in the field alone. It wasn't the safest thing to do, driving in cars with suspects, hanging out with them in bars and in their homes. I hadn't been trained in investigative procedure, so I'd fly by the seat of my pants. But this time, I invited fellow HSUS investigator Bob Baker to accompany me on my trip to the Midwest.

After flying to Illinois and then visiting the other Michigan slaughterhouses on my list, Bob and I headed east to Detroit. Bob drove the rental car, and I navigated. We had no trouble finding the run-down industrial part of town or the address of the plant. But, for some inexplicable reason, we couldn't locate the slaughterhouse. On that street, there were only boarded up brick buildings in a state of disrepair. We circled the neighborhood for half an hour, driving up and down adjacent blocks. I couldn't for the life of me figure out what was going on.

Bob finally pulled over in front of the address, I rolled down my car window and called out to the only man in sight. "Excuse me, sir," I said. He was ambling down the potholed street and walked over to our car.

"We're looking for B&J Packing?" I said with a question in my voice. "It's a slaughterhouse and it's supposed to be right here at this address. We were just wondering if you'd ever heard of it, or if you know where it is?"

"Oh, sure, B&J Packing? Yeah, it *was* right here. B&J Packing's been out of business goin' on three years."

Bob and I looked at each other in disbelief. Then it sunk in. We both knew Wills was an admitted con artist. But to what lengths was he willing to go? Had he wanted to impress his supervisors in the slaughterhouse meeting with his investigative prowess? Or was it just second nature for lies to come out of his mouth? He must have learned of B&J Packing during his Michigan

Humane Society days—whether the plant had had violations or not, we'll never know. Wills apparently was unaware that the slaughterhouse had been shuttered for three years, padlocks on the door.

And, thus, David Wills had staged an elaborate performance, replete with phone calls to his "informant." In short, he'd wasted our time—and HSUS donors' money—sending Bob and me on a wild hog chase that we would never forget.

Chapter 20

I was coming apart at the seams and didn't know where to turn. I was now extremely sensitive to light, and it seemed like whenever I went outdoors, my eyesight became grainy, I experienced visual overload, and a dull, pounding headache. I felt helpless, hopeless, and scared beyond words.

Thinking that my visual problem might in some strange way be connected to my OCD, I entered into an OCD clinical trial at the federal government's National Institutes of Health in nearby Bethesda, Maryland. There, a spinal tap was performed on me for research purposes, but, again, it yielded no definitive results.

Aware that suppressed feelings can often manifest as physical maladies, I wondered if my visual problem could be a function of my inability to fully experience my emotions. After all, growing up in a household rife with conflict—where Dad had punched a few holes in walls—expressing emotions had proved to be a liability. Likewise, when working undercover, I'd witnessed heartbreaking cruelty, all the while befriending the abusers with the requisite smile on my face. I was crazy about animals and yet, I was emotionally numb when getting spattered with brains while observing cow stunning, or when photographing horses being shackled, hoisted, and bled. Not surprisingly, I had erected an impenetrable fortress around my heart.

Repressed feelings have to come out some way, I surmised. Perhaps they were expressing somatically—that is, my emotions were manifesting physically.

Someone told me about Al-Anon, a twelve-step program for families and friends of alcoholics. Al-Anon is like the sister program of the more well-known Alcoholics Anonymous. There was, thankfully, no alcoholism in my family of origin. But to say that I was an alcoholic magnet in my dating life would be an understatement. It seemed like the partners I chose were all charismatic, charming, bad-boy alcoholics. I felt that through my choice of boyfriends, I qualified for Al-Anon. Thus, I thought, if I attended Al-Anon, I might get "in touch" with my feelings.

I'm not supposed to talk about Al-Anon here. Recovery programs like Al-Anon operate through attraction, not promotion. That's another way of saying that we aren't supposed to advertise twelve-step programs. Observers see how such programs have improved our lives, and, if they're so inclined, they'll organically want what we have. That said, I will keep my references to Al-Anon to a minimum. I'll simply say that the point of twelve-step programs is to understand that I don't control the universe. There is something bigger than me running the show. Bottom line: I'm not God.

It sounds presumptuous, I suppose. But that was a news flash to me. After all, for as long as I could remember, I thought it was my responsibility to somehow repair my parents' fractured marriage—a pattern of belief that extended far beyond my family of origin. When you come up in the world believing that you have control over things that are none of your business, it's hard to comprehend that you don't. Not surprisingly, I also concluded that it was my job—forgive the arrogance—to rescue the earth's animals. Endeavoring to "right size" myself, I started to attend twelve-step meetings a few times a week. Whether Al-Anon would benefit me remained to be seen.

Chapter 21

David Wills had made it abundantly clear that I was no longer to focus my efforts documenting slaughterhouse violations. He pronounced that, henceforth, all investigations were to be completed in eleven days. That, I was told, included my slaughterhouse case. This new policy upset me; I was not about to abandon countless cattle and hogs being disassembled and boiled alive. As much as my position at HSUS had been the culmination of my career dreams, with Wills as my boss, I felt I had been left with no choice but to resign.

The Humane Farming Association (HFA), headquartered in Northern California, had long been on my radar screen. That organization's signature campaign, the National Veal Boycott, had shed light on the horrors of calf production, resulting in a precipitous drop in numbers of veal calves slaughtered across the United States. *The New York Times* would ultimately call the veal campaign "the most successful animal rights boycott in the United States."[1] What's more, HFA had succeeded in getting the first state and federal legislation to protect farm animals introduced in the country and it operated Suwanna Ranch, the largest farm animal sanctuary in the United States. And, when it came to exposing factory farm abuses and attendant threats to human health, HFA did an end run around the media by placing full-page advertisements in newspapers nationwide and in magazines like *Time* and *Newsweek*. I knew HFA was a good fit for me.

When I spoke to Bradley Miller, the founder and national director of HFA, I learned that he was a caring, down-to-earth kind of guy. If I were to hire on at HFA, he explained, I would be given the means and support to continue documenting slaughterhouse violations. For starters, I would work out of my Maryland apartment, he said, with one inconsequential caveat: I would have to survive a three-month probationary period before my medical insurance benefits would kick in. Maybe leaving HSUS wouldn't be so bad, after all.

One evening, while shopping for some essentials at Bed Bath & Beyond, I saw a display of natural sea sponges and, not considering their animal source, I made the fateful decision to purchase one for the shower. I was accustomed to lathering up in the shower with a washcloth or my bare hands, but, on impulse, I purchased the loofa.

I showered with that sea sponge for months until a fissure developed down its porous center. Despite the split in the sponge, I continued to use it, the top piece bobbling from the bottom. When the sponge finally broke into two pieces, I tried showering with half. Half was too small and didn't do the job, so, one night, I tossed both pieces in the bathroom wastebasket.

The next morning, I would learn what a stroke of luck that had been.

It was the next in a list of providential happenings that would forever alter my destiny. For, I couldn't have known at the time that the simple act of tossing a sea sponge into the trash, compelling me to wash my body with my bare hands, would save my life.

Perhaps had I not showered with the sea sponge at all, my fingers would have detected the little hiccup in my breast months earlier. On the other hand, had the sponge not broken in half when it did, I likely would have been just another mortality statistic at the ripe old age of thirty-five.

Chapter 22

"It's cancer," the doctor informed me after performing a lumpectomy and having the specimen analyzed. I felt like my eyes were literally going to pop out of my head. Then, I was hit with a wave of fatigue.

Over the course of the next six months, if all went as planned, I would undergo chemotherapy—have chemicals injected or dripped into me—to kill off any straggling cancer cells in my body. Radiation would take six weeks. I would ride the DC subway to George Washington University Hospital daily where a huge X-ray-like machine would irradiate the area where the lump had been. And lastly, my treatment would be topped off with a five-year regimen of Tamoxifen, an antiestrogen drug.

The shock of the diagnosis wore off quickly, and numbness took its place. One thing was apparent to me: clearly, now was not the time to leave HSUS. My plans to work at HFA went up in smoke.

I had accumulated eight years' worth of medical leave from HSUS, and, with David Wills's approval, I decided to seize the moment and take time off. Not that I was going to sit at home and recuperate, as Wills assumed. On the contrary, between chemo treatments, I hit the ground running. Because Wills had effectively pulled the plug on my slaughterhouse investigation, I spent my sick leave flying from one slaughterhouse to another documenting clear violations of the Humane Methods of Slaughter Act—hardly the medical establishment's recommendations for patients undergoing cancer treatment. Unfortunately, I did have to cool my heels briefly in Maryland during most of that six-week stint of radiation therapy.

Two months into chemotherapy, in a small dressing room at George Washington University Hospital, I removed my dark blonde wig (I had lost my hair from the powerful chemotherapy) and pulled my T-shirt over my head. Next, I placed the wig back on my head to cover the few wisps of hair that remained. Sentimental about my hair, I hadn't wanted to cut those few lingering strands from my head, so I tucked them neatly under the cap of the shoulder-length wig. I covered myself with a white cotton gown which opened in the front and then walked to an area where the radiation oncologist and two radiation therapists stood waiting for me.

Alone, operating on autopilot, I just put one foot in front of the other. I felt nothing. Or, more likely, I couldn't afford to feel anything.

Told to remove the draping and lie very still on a rock-hard table, the therapists utilized special imaging—like a CT scan—to pinpoint the precise place on my chest where the radiation beam would, over the course of the next six weeks, be aimed. They used an instrument to tattoo two freckle-sized dots on my skin and then, with a special marker, drew large colorful Xs on my left breast—all designed to identify their target.

No radiation that first day, nothing upsetting, or so I thought. Just the mapping of my breast.

I left the university hospital and was driving my shiny Dodge pickup truck—black with thick orange and red stripes on the sides—the stripes reminiscent of the bold marks on my breast. Headed to another doctor's appointment, I encountered the usual heavy traffic traveling past Embassy Row on Massachusetts Avenue. I switched on my turn signal, and began changing lanes. Suddenly, inexplicably, I felt lightheaded. And then faint. I started seeing stars. It's one thing to pass out when you're stationary; it's another to faint behind the wheel of a moving vehicle.

As the wooziness overtook me, I managed to steer my truck into the first available parking lot. It was, of all places, the lot of the Vatican Embassy—the Embassy of the United States of America to the Holy See—an imposing three-story stone building, a red and white flag flapping in the breeze over the main entranceway. Growing increasingly weaker, I pulled into a space, put the vehicle in park, shut off the ignition, and opened the driver-side door. My panicked inclination was to let someone—anyone—know that I was in distress versus passing out alone in my truck. "I'm fainting!" I shouted to the only person in the parking lot. "I need help!"

A man, dressed professionally in suit, tie, and open overcoat, immediately ran to the truck, gently took my arm, and led me around the side of the impressive building, up a few steps, and in through the embassy's door. Once inside the structure, he called for assistance and a woman appeared. She ushered me into a formal drawing room and instructed me to lie on a plush velveteen couch. She kindly offered me some water, which I declined, and both she and the gentleman disappeared into the inner sanctum of the building.

Alone, in the dimly lit drawing room, windows cloaked in heavy draperies, I lay quietly for fifteen minutes trying to regain my composure. Here I was, reclining on a comfy sofa in the Vatican Embassy, of all places, a number of life-size, elaborately framed portraits of holy leaders—pious popes and bishops—dauntingly peering down at me from high up on the walls.

I'd thought the radiation therapists, massive X-ray machine, and mapping of my breast hadn't affected me in the least. I was wrong. They had taken a toll on my psyche. My fear had come out sideways.

After my short respite, I got my bearings and found the man and woman who had so generously helped me. I thanked them profusely for their aid and asked to use their phone. Although they encouraged me to rest a bit longer, I quickly called HSUS investigator Bob Baker to pick me up and chauffeur me the few blocks to HSUS. That evening, my dear friend Ellen, Dr. Michael Fox's administrative assistant, shuttled me back to my Maryland apartment; she wanted to make sure I got home in one piece.

I was still on medical leave from HSUS. With chemo well underway, and a one-week interval off from my radiation regimen, I flew out to a large California slaughterhouse to investigate a complaint. Despite being employed by HSUS, the Humane Farming Association generously footed the bill for my secret mission.

Depleted and barely able to stay awake, I soldiered on, documenting hogs being shocked by the stun operator three and four times; live animals left shackled and hanging from the plant's bleed rail while workers took their half-hour lunch break; and hogs jumping from the shackling table into the blood pit below, breaking bones, yet, like thousands of others, being hung up and immersed into the scalding tank alive.

With the blessing of my oncologist, I carried on board airplanes a cooler filled with syringes of costly serum to self-inject to boost my suppressed immune system. Even so, my skin hurt, my chemo-irritated eyes made it painful to blink, and my radiation-scorched lungs rendered it difficult to breathe. With each round of chemo, I grew sicker. I became so ill in one midwestern town that I was admitted to the hospital with what doctors suspected was a blood clot in my lungs, a potentially fatal side effect of chemotherapy. After extensive testing, a doctor concluded that I didn't have a blood clot, just a pair of seriously scarred lungs.

Chapter 23

Despite the fact that my lungs had been scarred, apparently from the radiation I'd undergone as part of my breast cancer regimen, I had been secretly traversing the country, going from one slaughterhouse to another. Now that my six-month treatment was over and my hair had started growing back, I knew it was time to return to HSUS and face David Wills. He had previously impeded my slaughterhouse work, depriving it of funding and requiring all investigations to be completed in eleven days. To help the slaughter-bound animals, I knew I'd have to leave behind what I'd considered my lifetime job. With Wills as my supervisor, I desperately wanted to quit.

But, if hired on as chief investigator with the Humane Farming Association, I would have to survive a three-month probationary period before HFA's medical coverage kicked in. And if I didn't make the grade at HFA, I would be in deep trouble—as a recent cancer survivor, it would be virtually impossible for me to secure medical insurance for myself. Wanting to be responsible, I couldn't take that risk. My hands were still tied: I had no choice but to continue working for David Wills for the foreseeable future.

On the first Monday morning in June 1992, I returned to work at the Humane Society's new suburban Maryland headquarters, a sprawling complex with lots of smoked glass and brick. Only the privileged few—the president and a handful of executives—had offices of their own. The rest of us worker bees were relegated to small cubicle workstations. Privacy gone, it was difficult to concentrate with phones ringing and employees talking all around.

For the next few months, with my slaughterhouse case on hold, Wills ordered me to do frivolous investigations that were quick, flashy, and accomplished nothing at all for the animals.

One summer day at lunchtime, I left the comfort of the air-conditioned headquarters to go outside for some fresh air. I sat down on a grassy knoll when, instantly, the heavy humidity caused my face and nose to swell. In a matter of seconds, I became disoriented and confused. My brain couldn't process the detail in the grassy clover patch—or in my surroundings—at all. It had happened thousands of times before, but on this occasion, perhaps exacerbated by the aftereffects of chemo and radiation, it seemed worse. I feared I would have to crawl back to headquarters on my hands and knees. I somehow held it together and made my way safely inside; my coworkers none the wiser.

I was so profoundly fatigued at the end of each workday that I could barely make the twenty-minute drive home. I fought with myself to keep my eyes open on Interstate 270, cars and trucks whizzing by. "What is wrong with you?" I asked myself. "Why are you so tired? Why are you doing this to yourself?" The chemotherapy and subsequent Tamoxifen had caused my hormones to plummet, triggering severe, soaking hot flashes; the radiation had permanently scarred my lungs and burned my skin. It didn't take a rocket scientist to comprehend the terrible toll my treatment had taken on my poor body and brain.

Back at the office, Wills now required his underlings to submit written logs of how we spent our time each day. Every minute, every phone conversation, every interaction had to be documented and accounted for. Wills, who was traveling to Africa on a junket, was going to micromanage us from half a world away.

Over the years, I had eaten, slept, and breathed HSUS, devoting my very being to the organization. I had proved myself a hardworking, conscientious, and highly productive writer and investigator. Now I was being treated like an employee who was neither trustworthy nor capable of doing her job.

A Fortress Around My Heart

Three months after my return to HSUS, when Wills arrived back from his African adventure, he informed me, in no uncertain terms, that my slaughter investigation was finished.

Knowing that farm animals were being skinned and boiled alive—with no one doing anything about it—was more than this body could bear. That week, taking a giant leap of faith, I submitted my letter of resignation.

I'd spent nine years at HSUS; yet when it came to my departure, there were no going away parties, no words of support. No one seemed to care. In the evenings when nobody was around, I quietly packed up my slaughter files and took them out to my truck.

I would be a recent cancer survivor with no medical insurance—it was just a gamble I'd have to take. Off to the Humane Farming Association I went.

And off to jail went Wills.

Shortly after my departure, David Wills was sued for sexual harassment by my former colleagues—his subordinates[1]—and prosecuted for embezzling from HSUS. He pleaded guilty to one count of embezzlement in Maryland Circuit Court and was sentenced to a six-month jail stint.[2] When he was released, he went to work for the opposition, the animal use industry.

But that wasn't the last we'd hear of David Wills. In time, he'd be tried in federal court in Texas for repeatedly sexually assaulting a young girl—from the time she was ten years old until she was thirteen. Wills had promised to pay the victim's college tuition, among other things, if her mother—Wills's mistress—allowed him to continue assaulting the child.[3]

Following the eleven-day trial, the jury deliberated for one day, convicting him of seventeen counts: one count of conspiracy to commit sex trafficking of a child; seven counts of sex trafficking of a child; eight counts of coercion/enticement of a minor; and one count of conspiring to obstruct justice.

This monster, convicted felon, and pedophile is now serving a life sentence in a Terre Haute, Indiana, maximum security federal prison.

This was justice, karma at its swiftest. While I don't wish harm on my worst enemy, I'll admit, I couldn't have been more pleased. After all, Wills had been living rent-free in my head for way too long. I could finally kick him to the curb.

Part Three

Animal Activist on the Loose

Chapter 24

HFA National Director Bradley Miller had the brilliant idea that if the media refused to expose my slaughterhouse findings, then perhaps I should write a book about them myself. And that was the genesis of *Slaughterhouse*.

I was busy compiling my interviews about animal cruelty, but I knew a book about slaughterhouse violations wouldn't be complete without also exploring dramatic increases in meat contamination rates, a direct consequence of the excessive production line speeds I'd documented. I interviewed parents whose children had accidentally consumed morsels of undercooked, tainted hamburger and had become permanently disabled or had died excruciating deaths from E. coli poisoning. I heard stories about three-year-olds who had been hospitalized for a few weeks to several months who had experienced gushing, bloody diarrhea and kidney failure, some ultimately suffering seizures, strokes, and massive heart attacks. I attended congressional hearings where mothers and fathers, clinging to framed photos of their deceased toddlers, recounted the harrowing details of just how the pathogen had invaded their loved ones' little bodies and slowly dismantled them organ by organ, until their children could no longer fight. I listened, transfixed, hanging on their every word. After all, these courageous, outraged parents had come to Congress to share their traumatic stories and shed light on the deadly toxins brewing behind the closed doors of slaughterhouses as a direct result of meat industry deregulation.

Nor would my manuscript be complete without examining the abuses to which the workers were subjected. My research revealed that slaughterhouse employees were routinely treated with almost as much disdain as the animal victims themselves.

I learned that meat and poultry packing represented one of the most dangerous industries the United States—with workers suffering tens of thousands of nonfatal and fatal injuries and illnesses a year. Employees had lost fingers, arms, breasts, and legs after they were dragged into equipment; had suffered miscarriages; had been burned, exposed to hazardous chemicals, stabbed, killed, and dropped dead on the line. Thanks to increased production line speeds, cumulative trauma disorders—which result from performing the same meat cutting motion as much as twenty thousand times a day—had skyrocketed.

Whether injured or ill, workers were required to visit "company doctors" who invariably sent them back to work before they were physically ready. Time and again, once they were back on the job, the company manufactured reasons to fire them.

Employees suffering from repetitive motion illnesses were rarely able to collect disability insurance, first, because they were often undocumented immigrants, and second, because company doctors claimed that they came to the job with the disorders. In short, packing plant workers were consistently chewed up and spit out—and left incapable of ever working again.

Taking a break from my research, I hopped a DC-bound subway to head to my annual gynecological appointment. Once there, the doctor conducted an exam and then left the room.

The glare from the fluorescent light overhead was killing me. It was hurting my light sensitive eyes and making my brain sizzle.

After a few minutes, the doctor returned. He said nothing until he was directly across from me. Then he looked down at his clipboard when he spoke.

"Well," he announced offhandedly, "it looks like your eggs are fried."

He spoke so dispassionately that I could not process what he had said. "What??" I asked, dumbstruck.

"I said, *it looks like your eggs are fried*," he repeated louder. "From the chemotherapy," he explained, his attempted glib pun ringing in my ears. My oncologist had never warned me that premature menopause was a potential side effect of chemo.

This was a gynecologist, for goodness sake. Surely, he would know better than to crack a joke when communicating such serious news. Looking back with a measure of compassion, I can now see that, not unlike me, this clinician had become distanced and detached; he'd walled himself off from me, perhaps a protective mechanism designed to keep patients and their problems at bay. Not surprisingly, there were no comforting words, no reassurances.

I stepped down from the exam table, gathered up my belongings, and made a beeline for the door. "See you next year for my annual," I said robotically, vowing to myself to never see this doctor again. Shell-shocked by his callous bedside manner, I walked to the Metro and boarded the train in a daze.

I continued visiting more slaughterhouses across the country. The *piece de resistance* was the world's largest hog kill. Located in Bladen County, North Carolina, the Smithfield plant killed a staggering 144,000 pigs a week, and had requested a permit to increase that number. It was described as a state-of-the-art facility, with animal chutes designed to reduce hogs' fear and distress. I tracked down one of the plant's stickers, a muscular African American man who spoke with deliberation.

"Does it ever happen that hogs are stunned improperly?" I asked the man.

"All the time," the worker responded. "Because if you're killing sixteen thousand hogs a shift, those guys aren't going to stun all the hogs all the time. Some hogs come out kicking and raising hell." Sometimes, he explained, hogs actually ran across the shackling table. When that happened, the shacklers often tackled the animals, hung them up by one leg, and sent them down the slaughter line alive. I probed further. When I asked if anybody had ever beaten hogs, the sticker answered, "That's all the time. You get a stubborn hog that doesn't want to go, they're going to beat that hog till he does. If the government's not around, which they're not, employees can get to beating that hog all they want to." He explained that oftentimes, supervisors used pipes to knock hogs down. But, to actually render them unconscious, he and his supervisors had to "hit them like you're hitting a baseball. You got to hit them across the head and knock them flat out."

I'd heard it all before.

Today, instead of using electricity to stun or kill hogs, the Smithfield plant in Tar Heel gasses hogs with cruel carbon dioxide.[1] The plant now has the capacity to kill an astounding thirty-five thousand hogs per day.[2]

Back at home in Maryland, I had a huge problem. Seated on my cane-backed chair at a table in my bedroom, I finished transcribing interviews, compiling affidavits, and I began the initial process of writing a book, typing away on my laptop for the better part of each day. The problem I experienced occurred when I *wasn't* typing. So focused was I on my writing, that when time came to call it quits each night, I looked away from my laptop, and, once again, I became disoriented. As if I were in a dream, my poor brain just could not process my environs. With my depth perception compromised and the rooms in my tiny apartment practically spinning, I felt like a drunkard. This would happen every night.

Compounding my problem was the fact that, ever since chemotherapy, and now on a five-year regimen of the antiestrogen drug Tamoxifen, my eyes had become very dry, puffy, and painful. What's more, I had become even more sensitive to light. When I drove at night, car headlights appeared fractured, with large halos trailing off in all directions. Even more troubling: when I would remove my glasses and peer at a light source, I could actually see a shower of cell-like structures raining downward.

"This thirty-six-year-old woman's history and problems are most unusual," wrote my Maryland ophthalmologist in a referral letter to the prestigious Johns Hopkins Wilmer Eye Institute. "Over the past twenty years, she has been easily overwhelmed by complicated visual stimulation. For example, when she goes into a shopping center, the numerous aisles, racks, etc., cause her to become disoriented. Over the past few years, this has become, she feels, debilitating.

"She has had 'visual training' in the past, with little response."

Animal Activist on the Loose

81

The referral letter landed me an appointment with Dr. Neil Miller, one of the world's leading neuro-ophthalmologists, who was practicing at Johns Hopkins. I drove the fifty miles to Baltimore. There, I underwent a battery of vision and neurological tests.

In his letter back to my referring physician, Dr. Miller summarized, "The patient states that she has had problems with visual perception since age thirteen. These problems have worsened over the last four years. She claims difficulty with depth, size, and spatial orientation. She describes the problems as an 'information overload' brought on by a variety of problems."

Dr. Miller went on to present the results of his neuro-ophthalmologic exam, which, with the exception of my red-green colorblindness, were unremarkable. My optic nerves were fine and my visual acuity stable.

"In summary," he concluded, "the episodic nature of the difficulties and the fact that they are induced by very specific environmental phenomena lead me to wonder if the patient may have some type of underlying seizure disorder." He then recommended that I have a PET scan (an imaging technique that shows the brain's ability to function) performed in which the environmental triggers that brought on the confusion be simulated in an effort to "localize the area of abnormality."

He was, in effect, suggesting that my problem might be more of a brain issue than something that was structurally wrong with my eyes. I did not pursue this very sensible avenue because such an expensive diagnostic tool was not covered by my medical insurance provider. What's more, I didn't think it would be possible to simulate the environmental stimuli that triggered my confusion during a PET scan. Besides, extreme glare and the accompanying shower of floaters had to be in the eye. It couldn't possibly be a brain thing, right? I had no idea of the important opportunity I was missing out on.

Chapter 25

I had never heard of "clenbuterol." But, thanks to two government informants, I was about to learn more than I ever wanted to know about the deadly drug. Clenbuterol, a highly toxic synthetic steroid-like drug, was being used by the US veal industry to stimulate rapid muscle growth in calves. It wasn't approved for use in the United States, with good reason; clenbuterol can cause increased heart rate, muscle tremors, headaches, dizziness, nausea, fever, chills, and even death in people who consume meat tainted with its residue.

Thanks to my first informant—Dr. Lester Friedlander, a former USDA veterinarian residing in Pennsylvania—I learned about a top-secret federal investigation into the veal industry's use of this black-market drug. Information about the smuggling of clenbuterol into the United States had been provided to the Food and Drug Administration (FDA) years before I ever got involved. Although the drug had been the subject of a major international crackdown in Europe, here in the States, the FDA was sitting on its hands. Since that time, US Customs had received a tip and had initiated its own investigation. Clenbuterol was found in the very first calf feed shipment that Customs intercepted from the Netherlands. That's where I came in.

The government's investigation had been done on the down low, and consumers had been kept in the dark. Acting on a tip from my second informant—a federal law enforcement agent who shall remain unnamed—I traveled to the Midwest and was able to locate just-unsealed court documents and piece together details of the investigation.

A staggering ten raids had been conducted by federal agents at the nation's leading veal facilities, and scores of feed manufacturers and veal calf farmers were under suspicion of criminal wrongdoing. Despite the fact that nearly 2 *million pounds* of clenbuterol-laced feed had already been sold to veal producers, the USDA—working hand in glove with the veal industry—was allowing the drug-tainted meat to flow freely into the food supply.

I was worried for consumers who ate this contaminated meat. After all, a few bites of veal and they could become very sick or even die. Yet, nobody in a position of authority was doing anything about it. I also was concerned for the poor calves; feed spiked with the illicit drug was known to increase the animals' heart rates and cause metabolic changes in their immature bodies.

I got on the phone to a food reporter I knew at the *LA Times*. "You're never going to believe this," I said, explaining what I had uncovered.

"Wow!" he said, at once appalled and enthusiastic. "Sounds like an incredible story. Send me whatever you've got," he said, providing me with the *Times*'s FedEx account number to ship the hundreds of pages of documentation I had amassed.

The reporter's story ran the following week,[1] was picked up by the wire services, and made news headlines throughout the country. Officials at the veal industry's national trade association stated in an internal memo that they feared "potential ruin."

In response to the widespread media coverage, USDA bureaucrats scurried to do damage control in an effort to convince the public that eating veal was "safe." They touted the results of a recent "study" in which USDA had collected tissue and organ samples from four hundred calves—that was four hundred out of seven hundred thirty thousand calves marketed that year—and tested them, using antiquated methods, for the steroid. USDA officials then reported their findings: the government hadn't found a single trace of the deadly drug.

Knowing from experience that USDA couldn't be trusted to do anything but protect the meat industry, I made what should have been a four-hour drive to northeastern Pennsylvania where Dr. Lester Friedlander lived. My eyes dry and swollen and my vision grainy, I became so fatigued while driving that

I had to pull over twice to nap. "Why are you so tired?" I badgered myself. "Why are you doing this to yourself?"

I arrived late on a cloudy Monday afternoon. Dr. Friedlander and I put our heads together and came up with a detailed plan: I would visit five calf slaughterhouses in Pennsylvania, New York, and Vermont, collect tissue and organ samples from already dead calves, and take them for analysis to a colleague who operated an animal drug testing laboratory at Cornell University in central New York.

Phoning the slaughterhouses from Friedlander's home, I used the cover that I was a college student conducting laboratory research and needed bladders and eyeballs from slaughtered calves. I knew that the bladders would likely be filled with urine, a good testing medium for clenbuterol. The illegal drug also accumulates in the animals' eyeballs, a reservoir that is essentially tamper proof.

Supervisors at the five slaughterhouses bought my story and agreed to provide the samples for a small charge. So far so good. Now I just had to visit the packing plants, with a Styrofoam cooler in hand, and pick up the goods.

The first "buy" went off without a hitch. I procured fourteen bladders and matching eyeballs, took them back to my motel room, laid them out on a plastic garbage bag on the bed, photographed them, and put them on ice.

The second purchase didn't go so well. I arrived at the slaughterhouse at the agreed upon time—six thirty on Wednesday evening. It was dusk and long after close of business—one-shift slaughterhouse operations usually begin in the early morning and wind down by mid-afternoon—and there were no workers in sight. I walked around the industrial facility, high ceilings, shackles hanging from an overhead rail, looking for the plant manager, or anyone, for that matter. My "hellos" echoed in the cavernous building, but no one responded. Eventually I found a small office, and was greeted by a man in his mid-fifties, sitting behind a large desk.

I had an uneasy feeling, being that there were only two of us in the plant; I just wanted to collect the body parts and be on my way.

On the phone, I had assumed the identity of a University of Pennsylvania student.

Animal Activist on the Loose

Introducing myself, I explained that I was there to pick up the samples. The man smiled, looked at me intently, said he had been waiting for me, and then cut to the chase. "You're not a student at the University of Pennsylvania," he said gruffly. "I've got contacts there. We looked you up. You don't go there. You're not even registered there."

I had to stick to my story, couldn't miss a beat. Not only did I want to leave this slaughterhouse in one piece, but I needed to buy some time. Having done my homework, I suspected that this man might be the plant owner, and possibly an officer of the veal industry's national trade association. I still had three more packing plants in the tristate area to collect organs from—and I didn't want him spreading the word about my scheme.

"I most certainly am," I replied, indignantly. "I go to Penn—I . . . I'll show you. I've got my student ID right here." I pulled my wallet from my purse and started to rummage through it, feigning surprise when I couldn't find my identification. "Well, it *was* here," I said with annoyance. "I must've left it back at the dorm." He almost seemed to believe me.

"I'll have to go back to Philly to get it," I said with irritation. "I'll bring it with me when I—uh, when I come back." I had to think fast. "I'll see you either tomorrow or Friday afternoon," I told him, asking him to keep the goods in the plant cooler until I returned.

He bought the story enough that I did not wind up hanging from a meat hook in the cooler myself. I got to leave his plant. Over the course of the next two days, as I furiously traveled to the remaining three slaughterhouses in Pennsylvania, New York, and Vermont, I called that plant owner from the road a few times, assuring him that I would be back to collect my samples, ID in hand, before the week was out. That bought me enough time to pick up a grand total of seventy-one bladder and matching eyeball samples before he could alert his fellow calf killers that an animal activist was on the loose.

Leaving the slaughterhouses behind, I drove up to central New York, where my Cornell University colleague conducted a preliminary screening on the samples I'd collected. He was humoring me, he thought, expecting negative results every step of the way. When a large number of the samples yielded positives, he suddenly refused to conduct the further testing necessary to confirm his results. I begged for an explanation. All I knew was that he wanted me out of his lab as quickly as I'd come.

Collecting the evidence had not been a cakewalk, but finding a laboratory willing to further analyze the samples would prove to be even more of a challenge. In short, no testing facility in the United States was willing to conduct mass spectrometry to confirm the presence of the controversial drug. After all, finding clenbuterol in veal calf samples would be tantamount to taking on the multi-billion-dollar meat industry. A few of the lab supervisors I spoke with stated, off the record, that they were concerned not only for business repercussions, but for their physical safety, as well.

Finally, I contacted chemists at a renowned food research institute in the Netherlands which operated the world's most sophisticated clenbuterol-testing lab. (Technicians there conducted thousands of clenbuterol tests annually as part of a certification program to keep Dutch veal ostensibly drug-free.) Eager to know about the clenbuterol problem in the United States, researchers there agreed to do the job. Carefully packing the samples on dry ice, I shipped them overseas via FedEx.

At a time when the USDA was assuring consumers that eating veal was safe, the Dutch chemists discovered that twenty-six of my seventy-one specimens—more than one-third of the samples—tested positive for the toxic drug. The Dutch chemists were shocked to have detected more positives in my small sampling than they had in years of testing hundreds of thousands of Dutch calves as part of their certification program.

Within days of receiving the results, my supervisor, Bradley Miller, and I booked flights to Milwaukee, Wisconsin, where the federal investigation into clenbuterol smuggling was based. Once there, we met with lawyers with the US Attorney's Office to turn over our conclusive findings. The attorneys were astounded and appeared mortified that a small nonprofit could pull off an investigation that the FDA, Customs, and USDA collectively could not. I was gratified that we were able to prevail where the federal government had so dismally failed.

Animal Activist on the Loose

Finally, I called *Primetime Live*, a network TV program hosted by veteran ABC news anchor Diane Sawyer. A producer there expressed interest in the story, so I shipped over a mountain of evidence and worked with her for months on end. She ultimately produced a powerful exposé on the industry scandal and government cover up, on which I appeared. All told, 18 million viewers learned the horrific abuses to which calves are subjected and the dangers of eating veal.

In the end, several veal industry leaders were convicted for their roles in the smuggling and distribution of a drug they'd deceptively labeled "Vitamin C." The operation's mastermind—the president of Wisconsin-based feed manufacturer Vitek Supply Corporation, whose month-long trial I attended in Milwaukee—was convicted of twelve felonies, sentenced to three and a half years in prison; his feed company was fined $1,000,000. Ten other veal industry kingpins were imprisoned for their roles in the conspiracy and/or forced to pay huge fines.

As for my "friend" at the calf slaughterhouse who suspected I wasn't a U of P student, I don't know what became of him. I imagine he wasn't all too pleased with the results of our investigation. Thanks to HFA's hard-hitting veal campaign, coupled with fallout from the television exposé and the media that swirled around the case, I'm happy to report that we've seen a staggering 89 percent drop in the number of veal calves produced in the United States in recent years.

Chapter 26

Driving around the Midwest, where I had been piecing together the government's clenbuterol smuggling case, my eye problem was, as usual, cause for concern. My symptoms kept mounting.

By now, I'd seen ophthalmologists, neurologists, neuro-ophthalmologists, allergists, endocrinologists, and psychiatrists, with no answers. I couldn't go on this way. Thus, while in Minnesota, I made a pit stop at the Mayo Clinic, located in the southeastern part of the state. Amazingly, without even an appointment—I was a walk-in patient at this world-renowned institution—I convinced a receptionist to squeeze me in for yet another assessment. A thorough eye examination was conducted. Everything checked out, so I was sent to the eighth floor for a neurology consult. There I was given a sedative, a sleeping EEG, and was deemed to be fine.

Well, sort of.

"Your neurological exam with me did not show any abnormality," wrote the neurologist in his follow-up letter to me. "An EEG was also performed. The study was normal." Contrary to the opinion I had received from the Johns Hopkins expert, he continued, "There was no evidence of a seizure disorder. I found no neurological disorder to explain your complaints." Once again, I was back where I had started.

The Mayo neurologist directed me to his colleague in another department, Psychiatry and Psychology. There, a physician conducted an in-depth evaluation and diagnosed me with a host of acronyms, everything from OCD to PTSD. He also threw in, for good measure, "depersonalization"—which is defined as the feeling that one is observing oneself from outside the body or has a sense that things are not real. (I was all too familiar with that terrifying sensation. I had experienced it on and off for thirty years.) Upon hearing

Animal Activist on the Loose 89

what I did for a living, the doctor smiled and looked me right in the eye. "You would be a psychoanalyst's dream," he said with a wink and a nod.

Surely these doctors knew what they were talking about. This, after all, was the esteemed Mayo Clinic. And, yes, I'd experienced anxiety in my life. Still, these diagnoses couldn't explain away my acute reactions to environmental triggers—such as various types of lighting, humidity, and allergies—or the shattered light and floaters that I now saw. And then, of course, there were the dots that I'd seen for as long as I could remember.

Chapter 27

My Maryland apartment was located twenty miles north of the nation's capital. The museums on the DC National Mall were terrific, but I rarely took time to visit them. Admittedly, I'd despised the crowds, traffic, and, most of all, the crime, when I'd first moved to the area thirteen years earlier to work for the Animal Welfare Institute. Since then, the congestion and crime had only gotten worse.

Over the years, I had squeezed in trips to Colorado and Oregon, and, then, most recently, to Montana, to scope out potential areas for me to live. In the northwest corner of Montana, just a stone's throw from Glacier National Park, I discovered a small A-frame cabin for rent. It was situated on a narrow spit of land jutting out into picturesque Flathead Lake, a thirty-mile-long body of water nestled amongst the Rocky Mountain pines.

With the Swan Mountain range and a channel of water brimming with mallards and river otters in the backyard, and the serene, satin-smooth lake in the front, I couldn't believe my good fortune in finding this place. A very noticeable bonus was the fact that the lack of humidity in Montana seemed to suit me by dramatically lessening the symptoms associated with my eye problem.

I phoned Bradley Miller from Bigfork and asked him if I could work from Montana. He thought about it for a moment, and then he said yes.

Packing up my Maryland apartment, I prepared to head west. First, I had to say goodbye to my small handful of friends.

It was my favorite restaurant in downtown Rockville; *was* being the operative word. Bombay Bistro served the finest South Indian food in the metro

DC area. It was my choice for a gathering of friends on a cold November night, a sendoff, a farewell dinner of sorts. In six days, I would be putting Maryland in my rearview mirror as I drove toward a much simpler life in snowy Montana.

Our dinner reservation at Bombay Bistro was for eight o'clock on Saturday night. A small upscale restaurant with Indian decor, the bistro had about fifteen tables and booths, cloth napkins folded like little tents at each place setting. My friends and I arrived within minutes of each other and were ushered to a table in the front of the restaurant.

The Indian beer was flowing freely, and the samosas and thali plate I ordered were scrumptious. Conversation with my friends was pleasant and animated. By the time 9:45 p.m. rolled around, most patrons had departed, leaving behind only our party of six and one other couple seated in a nearby booth. The evening was winding down.

Suddenly, the relaxed atmosphere was shattered as three men burst in through the café's side door. Wearing black ski masks and wielding weapons, they scuttled to the cash register and shouted loudly at the wait staff. "Open the register! Open the register!" they yelled. One man pointed his semiautomatic in the direction of the open kitchen; another aimed his gun at an Indian server dressed in all white.

Stunned, the server didn't react to their demand swiftly enough.

Pop! cracked the firearm.

I couldn't quite wrap my head around what was happening; it all occurred so fast. It took my brain a moment to register that the "pop" I had heard was the sound of gunfire. Only when I saw the server lying on the tile floor, his white pants bloodied crimson, did things begin to make sense.

Two of the gunmen stood at the register, waving their rifles and shouting at a cook in the open kitchen. The cook quickly ran to the register, opening it, and turning over the cash.

The third gunman had a different agenda. He positioned himself in front of our table and trained a pistol on me and my friends. "Stand up!" he hollered as he prepared to rob us at gunpoint, his face obscured by the ski mask, his eyes wild and intense.

On his command, we all immediately rose from our seats. Those on his side of the table knew only that a gun was pointed at the back of their heads.

Next, the assailant ordered us to sit down and then, strangely, to stand up again. He couldn't seem to make up his mind. While one friend later confided that she worried that blood spatter was going to stain her expensive white blouse, another blurted out, "What do you want us to do: stand up or sit down?" We thought her brashness was going to get us all killed.

"Gimme your wallets!" he demanded. We all reached into our purses, grabbing our wallets and handing them over to the man. After depositing them in his backpack, he reunited with his buddies and out the restaurant's front door they fled.

The police station was just a few blocks away, and, within minutes, the restaurant was swarming with cops. As they took our statements, we could hear the whir of a helicopter overhead, which was shining a spotlight looking for the thugs. EMTs tended to the waiter, who, as luck would have it, had only been shot in the leg.

It had been quite a farewell dinner, an extraordinary sendoff indeed. By the time the episode was reenacted on local television news in the Washington, DC, area, I was happily ensconced in my cozy A-frame a world away in Montana. The criminals were never caught.

Chapter 28

Instead of enjoying my new Montana home, I spent the better part of the next year completing my *Slaughterhouse* book. First, I extracted quotes from the scores of affidavits I had compiled, and, when that proved to be too dry, I listened to all the workers' taped interviews again, rewriting the manuscript using their actual jargon. It was an arduous, time-consuming task.

It had been a long, cold winter and spring, but as summer finally blossomed and the swallows took to flying over the channel out back, I yearned to be floating on an innertube on the lake in my front yard. But that was not to be. The publisher had set a December delivery date for the manuscript, which I had to meet, and I had not a moment to spare. I was essentially glued to my desk.

When finally published, *Slaughterhouse* was met with a resoundingly positive response. It gave me a unique platform to speak out on behalf of voiceless slaughter-bound animals. I travelled the country, giving presentations at colleges and at conferences. Attendees, even animal activists, were, for the most part, unaware of slaughterhouse violations. My radio interviews, some conducted in studio, others over the phone, reached listeners across the United States. In total, they were broadcast on more than one thousand radio stations. Newspaper stories reporting the violations I'd documented ran not only throughout this country, but also in India, Australia, France, Germany, Poland, Romania, and other nations around the globe. I was thankful for that. At long last, consumers were being forced to confront issues affecting farm animals and what these sentient beings had to go through to wind up on their dinner plates.

And then one afternoon at home in Montana, the telephone rang.

94 OUT OF SIGHT

"Hello."

"Hello, Gail?"

"Yes."

"It's Christine."

She needn't have identified herself; I'd have recognized that refined, cultured voice anywhere.

"I just finished reading *Slaughterhouse*," she continued. "I'm overwhelmed."

Could Christine Stevens actually be reaching out to me? *The* Christine Stevens. My former boss at the Animal Welfare Institute. The "mother of the animal protection movement," the "duchess of the defenseless." She was the erudite matriarch who reminded me of my authoritarian father, and around whom, fourteen years earlier, I had acted like a self-conscious jellyfish. She was the supervisor who I'd driven that hard bargain with when I'd resigned: I would continue trying to get animal stories published in national news outlets for AWI, but no longer expected to be paid.

Christine was also the woman who, working in lockstep with Senator Hubert H. Humphrey in 1958 (when I was only three years old), had successfully lobbied for and gained passage of the Humane Methods of Slaughter Act. In our conversation, Christine expressed deep disappointment over the fact that the law she had fought so hard to pass was going altogether unenforced by the USDA. She went on to say that she was grateful to me for my investigation and for exposing industrywide noncompliance with the act.

It was a full circle moment, and I was proud—and confident—when I spoke with her.

One morning a few weeks later, with my pride and confidence boosted, I had another unlikely phone conversation, this time while sitting on a hotel-room bed dressed only in my underwear. I was in Washington, DC, for a speaking engagement when I flicked on the television and flipped through the channels. I landed on CSPAN, where President Bill Clinton's secretary of agriculture was being interviewed. He concluded his remarks and the correspondent announced that the ag secretary would now take calls from the

Animal Activist on the Loose 95

viewing public. It was a golden opportunity for me to speak to this cabinet member and take his temperature on the slaughterhouse issue. I dialed the "liberal" call-in number several times only to get a busy signal. When I phoned on the "conservative" line, I got through.

"Mr. Secretary, my name is Gail Eisnitz and I am author of the book *Slaughterhouse*," I said. "My question to you is, well, during the course of my investigation, I spoke with slaughterhouse workers as well as your USDA federal meat inspectors inside slaughterhouses—individuals who represented over 2 million hours on the kill floor. I basically learned that due to the incredible consolidation in the meat industry and the incredibly fast line speeds in these operations, workers are routinely being forced to skin, strangle, beat, drown, and dismember animals while they are still fully conscious."

I took a breath.

"Now, it's my understanding that according to the inspectors themselves, they are virtually powerless to enforce the Humane Methods of Slaughter Act, and one of the reasons is because they are nowhere in the area of the plant where the animals are actually being slaughtered. Representative George Brown Jr. from California has written you a letter requesting an increasing in staff so that inspectors could be located in the plants where the animals are being slaughtered which is a requirement of the Federal Humane Methods of Slaughter Act.

"Your comment?"

The secretary responded. "I've read parts of your book and many people in the USDA have, as well. We are responsible for administering this act and I will take your concerns back to the people in the USDA responsible for it.

"We do, however, say our prime function at these slaughter plants is food safety," he deflected, "to make sure that the product that goes through the plant is safe. And within the money that Congress gives us," he continued, "the appropriated monies for our inspectors who do this extraordinarily good job of making sure that the food is safe, there is no question that they are stretched in terms of their responsibilities. So I understand your point.

"I'll talk to the relevant folks at USDA about this. I do think it's important to recognize that with our food safety system relying on our outstanding inspectors, together with a better use of science, we are improving every day the safety of the food that is out there in the marketplace."

Enough said. This meat industry mouthpiece had answered my question with a non sequitur, failing to address the issue I'd raised. The USDA's priorities were unambiguously clear. That was all I needed to know.

Chapter 29

Back in Montana, the glare of the Big Sky sun was getting worse; light that reflected off car windshields was almost blinding; my night vision was shot; the accompanying shower of floaters was cause for concern; and I was getting pounding headaches several times a week. The dots or pixelated vision of my youth persisted, and there was, at times, a shimmering effect across my entire visual field. I *knew* I wasn't imagining this.

Because I was traveling to Los Angeles to do a spate of in-studio radio interviews, I scheduled an appointment at the prestigious UCLA Jules Stein Eye Institute. I was as determined as ever to get to the bottom of my eye problem.

It wouldn't be the first time I'd have electrodes placed in my eyes to measure the electrical activity of my retina in response to a light stimulus. The first time had been at Georgetown University Center for Sight in Washington, DC, where the results were inconclusive. Now, at UCLA's Jules Stein Eye Institute, because the ophthalmologist I saw noted that red-green color blindness in women is uncommon, I was referred to one of the leading retina specialists at the impressive facility. At his direction, a research ophthalmologist conducted another Electroretinogram or ERG.

The doctors' conclusion: "ERG responses are moderately abnormal for both eyes, with the left eye worse than the right. Both rod- and cone-mediated vision are affected . . . Overall, these results are consistent with mild to moderate panretinal abnormalities." The results suggested that I had "cone dystrophy."

Cone dystrophy is a rare eye disorder that affects the cone cells in the center of the retina. Cones are a type of photoreceptor cell that give us our color vision. They help us see fine details. What's more, they respond to different light wavelengths, and function best in bright light. Cone dystrophy can cause decreased visual acuity, decreased color perception, and increased sensitivity to light.

At long last, we were on to something. But it wasn't a good something. Could this explain my acute reactions to environmental triggers such as detail, humidity, and dim light? Could this be the cause of my headaches, my visual confusion? Was I going to lose my sight?

Part Four

Giving Voice
to the Voiceless

Chapter 30

It was quite fortuitous that I was now living in Montana. After all, Montana was, relatively speaking, just a hop, skip, and a jump away from a large cattle slaughterhouse in southeastern Washington State where workers were striking over line speeds. It would be a mere eight-hour drive from my home in Bigfork to the strikers' picket line. I got in my car and headed west.

The rolling hills of southeastern Washington were vast with wineries and famous Walla Walla onion fields. It was a windy June day when I arrived in Wallula, Washington, on the Columbia River, the site of the Iowa Beef Processors plant, better known as IBP. The Teamsters Union was striking over stalled contract negotiations, deplorable working conditions, lack of USDA oversight, and, as mentioned, a line speed that moved so fast workers could not perform their jobs adequately.

The rank and file—nearly eight hundred workers, most of whom were Hispanic immigrants—maintained the picket line. Slaughtering had come to a dead halt.

The rally cries along the picket line—located on an access road next to the slaughterhouse—were shouted in Spanish. Mexican and American flags blew in the breeze. Placards in English read, IBP: WE NEED SLOWER CHAIN SPEEDS and USDA—STAND UP FOR CONSUMERS AND WORKERS!

A Latina woman with her hair clasped under a baseball cap stood outside a small trailer near the picket line. On a table outside, I saw a recent *New York Times* article about this woman's fight for reform at the plant.[1] It turned out that she had walked off the production line when a fellow employee had been unable to keep up with the rate of production. She and a few dozen workers had followed the employee into the supervisor's office where they were all immediately fired. In no time flat, hundreds of people had staged a spontaneous walkout and were rallying outside the plant. IBP chained the doors shut to keep the remaining employees inside.

After explaining to the woman who I was, I found myself sitting inside the tiny trailer interviewing and audiotaping witnesses who had congregated outside the door. Among other things, the strikers were trying to expose the USDA's lack of regulatory oversight over contaminated beef. If line speeds were so fast that the USDA couldn't enforce meat safety laws, I suspected humane slaughter regulations would be a casualty, as well.

One of the picketers, a bilingual Hispanic woman whose job was cleaning out cows' intestines, agreed to interpret for me. In fact, she consented to be my first interview.

She complained that there were only two bathroom stalls available to accommodate from seventy-five to one hundred employees. With a fifteen-minute break, workers often couldn't go to the bathroom; they had to resume work because their time was up.

"People who can't hold it just go on the production floor," she said. "There's a guy that's working in there now, in the cooler, he can't leave his job and he uses the 'rest room' right in the cooler. After he goes, he doesn't wash—there's nothing to wash your hands with."

"He just pees in the cooler?" I asked.

"Yeah. Then he goes back to work like nothing," she said.

Another worker, a man nicknamed Flaco (Spanish for "skinny"), was listening in on our conversation and suddenly added his two cents in broken English. One of his friends, he explained, asked repeatedly for permission to go to the bathroom. "The supervisors, they just ignoring him and he work in packaging. So he grab a bag, and pee in the bag by the production floor."

"Most of the women in there, they wear pads," my translator said. "Everyday. Because there's times that they can't go to the rest room and they can't hold it.

"There's a lot of stuff where product falls on the floor," she continued, "and the supervisor just checks to be sure that the USDA inspector's not watching, and then just sticks it back on."

Giving Voice to the Voiceless   103

"The peoples that sweep get the meat and pile it up to put it in the [inedible] barrel," said Flaco. "I seen supervisors go and pick up meat from that pile. Meat that's already swept with all the guck in that pile. And they throw it back on the line."

In the past, Flaco added, employees wore frocks that had outside pockets where workers would store their tissues. "Now they don't have pockets no more. So now there's peoples that just wipe their boogers on their gloves."

My interpreter started up again. She said that at the "back hoof"—the station where a worker removes one of the cow's lower hind legs—a cow was kicking and accidentally amputated a worker's three fingers. "The cows are kicking and jumping and everything. And the company didn't save the fingers, so the worker lost them." Company management waited a short period, and then fired the worker.

This was my opening. After all, I felt bad for the worker, but my focus this day was on humane violations, and I wanted to determine whether cattle were still alive and conscious at the "back hoof."

When asked, she explained that she had worked "light duty," painting, and she'd seen workers kicked by live cows. "It's not the nerves," she said, as if reading my mind. "They're alive. I've seen when they stick them and they're not bled all the way, when they start skinning them is when they start coming back to life.

"Sometimes the knocker knocks the cows, and when he opens the door [to the worker who shackles the animals], the cows stand up and start running. Because there's no time to knock them right.

"Every day they go alive. Lots of times. When they open them up is when they start making noises."

"When they skin them?" I asked.

"When they skin them. When they skin the arms, or when they cut the hooves off."

"And they make noise?"

"They make noise."

My next interview confirmed that fact. José, a short, muscular man, removed hide from the cow's hindquarter and was stationed after the "first legger." He did not speak English. I asked my interpreter if José had ever seen improperly stunned cows that were still alive after knocking. She posed the question to him.

"Yeah," she responded. "Because even when they are taking the skin off the cow, they're still alive, you can hear them like 'Mrrrrr.'" José mimicked a cow's low groan.

"And are they still alive when they reach him?"

"Yeah. That's what he said right now. That when he's trying to peel them around, they're still alive and moving. He says that sometimes they go pretty far, sometimes they have all the skin out, they're all peeled."

"What makes him think that they're still alive?"

"He said you notice them because they're making noises and when they try to stick the knife into the cow, they're trying to kick. And if you look at their eyes, you can see the tears of a cow, and their eyes are moving and everything."

As distressing as it sounded, this was not news to me. I'd documented this time and again at other beef plants. But it was critical information to have on audiotape if we were to build a solid case against IBP.

Next in the queue waiting to speak with me was a slender man with slick black hair. As "gutter," Antonio opened up the cow's abdominal cavity far down the slaughter line, after the animal was dead. "The reason he's seen the live cows is they assign him to do cleanup. So, he's able to walk around."

A loudspeaker outside, amplifying festive trumpet music, was making it difficult to hear my interpreter.

As gutter, he said, he encountered a lot of pregnant cows. "He thinks the saddest thing is when he opens the stomach and the babies come out alive. He says there are baby calves in there that are waiting to be born. He's got to pull out the baby. They already have their hands sticking out. So, he has to cut the cow open so he can pull the legs out to take out the calf. They take the blood out of the baby calves, and they sell that blood for a lot of money."

I knew that these calves were called "slunks" and that their blood was used for biomedical research. I'd recruited an employee at another plant to shoot videotape of the blood-extraction process. To an average viewer, I suppose it would have been difficult to watch; to me, still detached and numb, it was just part of the job.

"Anyway, they put the babies in a grinder. It's cutting them, it's grinding them. It's called a worm. They go into dog food."

I asked again if he ever saw workers hang cows up while still alive.

"He said it's not just the kicking that makes him think the cows are alive. They're yelling, and you can see their eyes popping out."

Over the next several days, I would interview a few dozen kill floor employees. One man, in his late fifties with a cigarette hanging from his lips, had been a knocker at the plant for nine years. He explained that, because cows would not readily enter the knocking box, to expedite the slaughter process and keep shackles full, workers were excessively prodding the animals in the kill alley. That rendered them frantic by the time they reached him. Allowed to use only one bullet in the captive bolt gun per animal, and under extreme time pressure, he estimated that he successfully stunned only *five or six cattle out of every twenty* he shot. And while the sticker was armed with a backup knocking gun, he didn't have time to use it.

"The USDA needs to stop the chain!" the knocker exclaimed in broken English. "The chain don't stop. It keeps running."

Because cows were balking at the knocking box, he said, workers equipped with electric prods shocked them relentlessly. As a result, the cows "come inside the knocking box jumping, moving, put their heads down, coming up! I need thirty or forty seconds or a minute for one hit." Required to knock more than three hundred cows per hour, he literally didn't have time to kill.

"And the supervisors say, 'Keep knocking! Keep knocking! You need cows on the line!' Knocking the cow's ear is not very good." I knew a captive bolt gun to the ear would not render a cow unconscious.

A tractor-trailer drove by, blasting its horn in support of the picketers; the strikers hollered and waved back.

In his position as knocker, he rotated jobs with the shackler, where he had to hang live, conscious cattle. "Supervisors yell, 'Take it up! Take it up!' I need to put the shackle on it! The cow is alive and I pull him up."

Finally, as with the others, I asked him what the cows were doing that made him think they were alive. He imitated the animal by huffing and puffing heavily through his mouth.

"It's breathing?" I asked.

"Yeah, the blood no coming out. The cow can go ten minutes sometimes, and the cow will go still alive. All the people can open the legs, the stomach. Moving. Move the eyes. The nose. Look around. Look around."

Every employee shared similar details of conscious cattle, each a version of the same story. While some described the dangers that live, kicking cows posed to workers—"Many accidents because of that!"—others said faulty stunning equipment made it impossible for them to do their jobs.

The last employee I would speak with on this, my first, visit to Wallula, had worked as "second legger" for eight years. At about six feet, he was the tallest of the men I'd interviewed; he was slim with a narrow face and deep brown eyes.

He independently corroborated what the knocker had told me. "He says the cows can get ten minutes down the line and still be alive," my interpreter explained. "By that time, everybody's been doing his part, and you got fifteen workers already endangered. All the hide's stripped out all the way down to the neck there. He said they've been up to the 'down puller' still alive.

"He says as workers, they can do nothing about the live cows," the translator continued. "If he sees a live cow, he can't stop the line. Because the supervisor has told him that you can work on a cow that's alive.

"At the beginning, it was very hard to work on live cows. But within time, you get used to it. Because it's your job, and you have to do it. He says working on live cows is normal to him now, because he's done it for so long."

Giving Voice to the Voiceless 107

In all, I'd interviewed knockers, shacklers, stickers, leggers, butters, flankers, and a host of other kill floor workers. Never in my career had I had access to so many slaughterhouse employees so willing to speak to me simply because they believed it was the right thing to do. At Kaplan Industries in Florida, it had taken days of visiting bars and cafes, convenience stores and trailer parks, to locate a single eyewitness. And once I'd met that witness, I'd have to spend time coaxing him to talk and reassuring him. At IBP in Wallula, I felt like I'd hit the mother lode.

Speaking of Florida, Kaplan whistleblower Timothy Walker was never off my radar, and rarely far from my thoughts. I checked in with him from the road weekly; me, keeping him apprised of my investigations, he, aghast at my revelations and shoring me up. Tim was always only a phone call away.

Chapter 31

It was a relief getting home, but I knew I wouldn't be using the kayak I had finally purchased anytime soon. I had far too much work ahead of me. HFA had rented a small office for me, and I could hardly get there fast enough to start transcribing tapes. I used a foot pedal-operated transcription machine and listened with headphones as I typed on my computer keyboard. The way I saw it, every day I spent transcribing was a day that more cows were being skinned and dismembered alive. Every minute counted.

The Teamsters' strike was settled after a month's time, unsatisfactorily for the workers who won a wage increase at the expense of their pension plan.

Next, I had to write up affidavits for each worker, another time-consuming task. The weight of the job was not lost on me; I seemed to be getting sicker by the day. The eye problem was gaining ground. Now, whenever I walked the quarter mile to my office in town, I invariably ended up with grainy vision, confusion, and a migraine headache. I kept the overhead lights off in my workspace and typed by natural light from a small window.

As the affidavits were completed, I sent them to a court certified interpreter who then translated them into Spanish and FedExed officially stamped copies back to me.

I then arranged for a whistleblower attorney to fly in from Seattle to meet with me, the witnesses, and their family members in the honeymoon suite of a motel near Wallula. The attorney, through a translator, explained to the workers that, thanks to a retainer agreement with HFA, he would represent the employees should IBP retaliate against them for their whistleblowing activities. He asked each worker to sign a contract with him, and they *did*.

Giving Voice to the Voiceless

I almost keeled over. Never had I seen such brave and motivated workers. My hope renewed, my faith in humanity restored, my gratitude overflowed.

It had taken months of preparation to get all the affidavits written up, translated, and ready for signing. And it would take more time—and more trips to Wallula—to document *ongoing* violations and to get these and additional affidavits signed. What's more, I was now working two different angles. First came the affidavits, and second, the videotape.

"It would be easier to get a hidden camera into a maximum-security prison than into a slaughterhouse," said Mitchell Wagenberg, a New York City manufacturer of covert cameras, after I had told him the limitations we were facing. After all, the workers couldn't bring anything onto the kill floor with them; they were equipped only with tools like pneumatic knives and hydraulic cutters. Compounding that problem was the fact that their lockers were inspected, and their pockets and pants legs were searched at the end of each day to make sure they were not stealing meat. A few workers and I strategized with Wagenberg, who ultimately designed the perfect setup: a camera built into a stopwatch, which workers were allowed to carry onto the kill floor to time the disassembly process. The videographer would also have to wear the recording unit in a jockstrap. A courageous employee was trained to use the camera, and finally, we were in business.

The video he shot depicted panicked cows jumping wildly as they were prodded into the knocking boxes. Cows who fell down in the kill alley were trampled as workers forced other cows to run over them. A downed cow was chained at the neck and dragged alive into the knocking box. Another, who had reared up and fallen onto its back in the knocking box, had an electric prod jabbed into and held inside its mouth—the workers' futile attempt to right the cow and keep the production line moving swiftly.

Once in the knocking box, cows were repeatedly struck with ineffective knocking guns, in some cases falling to the ground and struggling to their feet after the attempted stun. In other instances, the knocking gun became embedded in cows' skulls while the dazed animals remained standing. And finally, and most importantly, the video showed thrashing cows who had been shackled and hoisted upside down on the bleed rail and were still alive as they proceeded to the sticker, belly ripper, tail ripper, and on down the line. These cows were trying to right themselves, snorting, their eyes blinking and bulging and their tongues jutting out. In all, I tallied one hundred violations in the three and a half hours of video we had obtained. It was a relief to know we had finally gotten the goods; we had the evidence necessary to make a strong case.

Chapter 32

Duane Pohlman, chief investigative reporter with the NBC-TV affiliate in Seattle, had read *Slaughterhouse* and had contacted me about the possibility of someday producing a segment on packing plant violations. Now was the time to reach out to him.

"Boy, Duane, have I got a story for you," I said, and we discussed the IBP case in detail. A meticulous and thoughtful reporter, he was all over the story. I sent him all the raw videotape footage the worker had shot at IBP. I then traveled to Wallula to assist Pohlman in conducting on-camera interviews with the workers for his upcoming story.

When his first story aired (he would produce a total of twelve segments), thousands of letters and emails of gratitude poured into the station.

Two days after Pohlman's first story aired, at IBP's request, the company's paid humane slaughter consultant, Dr. Temple Grandin, visited the plant. There she documented—even with advanced warning and a reduced line speed—such unacceptable handling practices that she was forced to flunk the plant on her entire audit. Despite this, the following week, in a *Seattle Times* story, an IBP spokesman stated, "A livestock expert paid by the company toured the plant last week and found no improprieties in cattle handling."[1] It was the first in what would become a pattern of practiced, bald-faced lies.

"Just going there and watching that plant, you can see it has big problems," Grandin shared with me in a phone call a few days after her visit. She went on to say that the "atrocious" conditions and violations at IBP were not the fault of the workers—something I'd been proclaiming all along. Had the company hired her to view HFA's video before her inspection, Grandin said, she would have flunked the plant on the basis of the tape alone.

Next, with a one-two punch, two plant workers and I conducted a Seattle press conference and petitioned then-Washington Attorney General Christine Gregoire—the top law enforcement official in the state—to criminally prosecute IBP management. Adding weight to our effort was the fact that a representative of the National Joint Council of Food Inspection Locals (NJC)—the federal meat inspectors' union—spoke at the news conference, joining with HFA in seeking to prosecute IBP. In a statement to Attorney General Gregoire, the vice chairman of that union wrote, "The NJC is petitioning Attorney General Gregoire to enforce state laws similar to those that fall under our purview. We believe that is the only way to ensure compliance with humane slaughter requirements."

Never before had federal meat inspectors joined with animal activists in calling for a criminal investigation of a slaughterhouse by state authorities. The USDA's own inspectors were publicly announcing that they were unable to enforce the federal Humane Methods of Slaughter Act—and they were calling on the state to step in and enforce local humane slaughter laws. HFA no longer had to fight the battle alone. I couldn't have asked for better reinforcements. The meat inspectors themselves had come to our aid.

If that wasn't enough, HFA ran full-page advertisements in newspapers throughout Washington State, urging readers to contact the Attorney General. Accompanying a photo of a panicked steer with terror in his eyes, the headline read:

**HE'S BEEN SKINNED ALL THE WAY TO HIS HEAD
HIS LEGS HAVE BEEN CUT OFF
. . . AND HE'S STILL CONSCIOUS.
ONLY YOU CAN STOP IT.**

While Attorney General Gregoire claimed that she didn't have legal jurisdiction in the case, the governor of Washington stepped in and appointed a multi-agency task force to investigate. Ironically, he put Gregoire in charge of the task force.

Giving Voice to the Voiceless 113

"This is the first time in US history that a governor anywhere has called for a full-scale investigation of slaughterhouse practices," reported the NBC San Francisco affiliate covering the story. We were indeed making history. I felt optimistic and energized about the case.

And then IBP mounted its defense.

Plant management scurried to do damage control, first issuing a press release claiming that the videotape was staged by workers and that USDA inspectors were present in the slaughter areas "100 percent of the time." Next, executives from IBP headquarters interrogated workers, engaging in a campaign of terror to ferret out the videographer, suspending and firing whistleblowers, and threatening others with jail time. Uninterested in the skinning and dismembering of live cattle at the plant, company officials were laser focused on their security lapse.

In a shocking turn of events, during a teleconference with HFA's Bradley Miller and me, a member of the governor's task force suggested that the entire case amounted to a single misdemeanor count "worth maybe $250." Another task force member, the county prosecutor, proposed that the whistleblowers, because they had participated in the offenses, be the *target* of the investigation.

What? You've got to be kidding, I thought. Bradley and I challenged their ludicrous proposal, their attempt to scapegoat the workers, but the bureaucrats on the phone wanted nothing to do with our defense of the courageous employees.

The writing was on the wall.

Aware that the governor's task force was doing everything in its power to protect IBP, HFA ran another ad exposing the governor for his role in the coverup. The governor's office was flooded with mail.

Next, an NBC *Dateline* producer, who I'd been funneling information to for many months, sent a correspondent and camera crew out to Wallula to cover the story. With an interpreter and our whistleblower attorney at their side, twelve employees bravely bared their faces on camera. They described in vivid detail what it was like to butcher cows when they were still alive.

But, true to the media's form, the story never saw the light of day. Just as ABC and CBS had failed to air stories about slaughter violations a few years earlier, NBC went a step farther, actually taping the interview with workers, and then, weeks later, killing the exposé with no explanation at all.

As months passed, and the state intensified its defense on behalf of the slaughterhouse, cattle continued to be skinned and dismembered alive. I produced another twelve worker affidavits demonstrating that problems persisted.

Eight months into the State's investigation, *The Oregonian* newspaper published a cover story in which a plant employee stated that he still observed cows being dismembered alive. According to the article, "He mimicked their antics, rolling his head and torso and blinking. He estimated one animal struggled for ten minutes. 'This cow had no back feet and seventy percent of its skin gone, and it had to be stunned again,' he said through a Spanish speaking interpreter."[2]

The culmination of the task force's disinformation campaign came when the state outrageously alleged that HFA had "manufactured" the videotaped evidence.

Almost a year after we had gone public with the violations, the task force bumped the case down to the county prosecutor—whose sheriff's office was suddenly awarded $5,000 for patrol car camera equipment by IBP.[3] In his decision letter, the prosecutor announced that he was not filing charges against IBP. Instead, he mounted a vigorous defense on behalf of the slaughterhouse, contending that HFA's documentation "was produced not by a neutral and detached law enforcement investigation, but by an organization and individuals who *manufactured the evidence in order to fulfill their own agendas*." The flabbergasting result: According to the task force's final report, *all evidence developed by HFA was discredited*.

Newspapers blanketed Washington State declaring that the county prosecutor had refused to file charges at IBP because HFA had purportedly fabricated evidence. "No Charges in Livestock Handling Investigation," read an IBP news release. "A state investigation into allegations of livestock mishandling at IBP's Wallula, Washington, beef plant has resulted in no charges and confirmed that animal rights activists 'manufactured' evidence against the company."

History was repeating itself. Just as the US Secretary of Agriculture had issued outrageous lies to protect Kaplan Industries in Timothy Walker's Florida case, now, members of the governor's task force were spinning falsehoods to shield IBP.

I would eventually obtain the task force's internal communications and investigative documents through Washington's Public Disclosure Act (PDA). Among those records was an interview with Dr. Temple Grandin, IBP's humane slaughter consultant, who said that the plant's dilapidated facilities were making cows balk and back up—causing a significant delay per animal. Workers, struggling to keep shackles full, were therefore excessively prodding cattle, resulting in panicked animals entering the knocking box. She concluded, "The knocking box and facilities in general are borderline falling apart and overloaded. . . . Even when things are going well at IBP," she said, "it still doesn't go good."

Also released under Washington's Public Disclosure Act was an internal memo drafted by the attorney general's office five months *before* the county prosecutor declined to file charges. It was a roadmap for the state to follow to defend its preordained decision to not prosecute IBP. According to the memo, the attorney general's office intended to "deliver a message questioning the credibility and sincerity of HFA" and allege that "animal cruelty charges had been orchestrated for fundraising purposes."

Also obtained under the PDA was a fifteen-page document prepared by a law firm retained by IBP and marked as "Privileged and Confidential Work Product." It was released to the county prosecutor and inadvertently to us. This "draft timeline" described numerous incidents in which workers had been unable to stun cattle properly or were "allowing hot beef to pass the sticker area." What a smoking gun that was—effectively implicating corporate management for its knowledge of and culpability in the problem!

And finally, although humane slaughter regulations require that stun operators be well trained, stunning equipment be carefully maintained, and animals be rendered insensible to pain with a single application of the stunning device, the Washington State Patrol officer assigned to write up the final report saw fit to disregard those "minor" details. His investigative conclusions, also obtained under the PDA—which ultimately helped inform the prosecutor's decision—stated that "the incidents appearing on tape and the problems detailed in witness statements and interviews appear to stem from two sources: inadequate training and supervision and facility and tool maintenance *instead of a blatant disregard for the law* [emphasis added]."

In all, we obtained hundreds of pages of records under the PDA. They documented a carefully choreographed scheme in which task force members knowingly, calculatedly, and deceptively issued fabrications—*and willfully conspired*—to mislead the public about the ongoing violations at the plant and protect IBP. It would take an entire book to fully expose the magnitude of corruption we encountered and the extent of the state's cover-up.

IBP had escaped prosecution but, fortunately, all was not lost. First, during the course of the investigation, we generated widespread media coverage of the violations on television and in newspapers throughout the western United States. Second, the whistleblowers informed me that IBP's plant manager and several kill floor supervisors were fired from their jobs for their roles in the violations, and McDonald's, a major IBP client, suspended the plant for thirty days. Third, the company installed video cameras on the kill floor. And, last but not least, IBP management agreed to allow the Washington State Department of Agriculture to conduct so-called unannounced inspections of the plant's premises for a year and a half.

While I was encouraged to hear from workers that major structural improvements made to the drive alleys and stunning areas resulted in a precipitous drop in the number of cows being butchered alive, I remained dubious. After all, it was IBP's production mentality and exorbitant line

Giving Voice to the Voiceless 117

speeds that had caused the violations in the first place. These issues hadn't changed at all.

Months later, IBP, Inc., the nation's largest red meat processor, was purchased by Tyson Foods, Inc., for 4.7 billion dollars. Today, Tyson is the second largest processor of poultry, pork, and beef in the world.

As for Attorney General Christine Gregoire, she was never held accountable. On the contrary, she was rewarded for turning her back on the workers and the animals. Had she been exposed for covering up what would have been the biggest meat industry scandal ever to have hit that state (I begged the *Seattle Times* to run the story), it would have cost her dearly. For the final vote was the closest gubernatorial race in US election history. Out of 2.8 million ballots cast, when a statewide hand recount was conducted, Gregoire beat her opponent by 129 votes.[4] Christine Gregoire was awarded the governorship of the State of Washington, a position she held for two terms.

As for me, to say that I felt devastated and deeply betrayed by the criminal justice system would be an understatement. Not only did it seem like all my hard work had gone up in smoke, but now we were labeled "evidence manufacturers" by the very people who were supposed to enforce the law. I knew that no matter what I said or did, these "authorities" would never listen to me. They had their own agendas. I felt as powerless as the animals I was supposed to be protecting.

Chapter 33

I didn't have many friends in Montana. After all, who had the time? I was busy working. I would attend the occasional twelve-step meeting, but, in Bigfork, a town of three thousand, only two to four members would show up. The meeting eventually closed from attrition. I was lonely, obsessed with my slaughterhouse work, and getting sicker by the day.

One highlight of my austere existence was my weekly telephone call with Timothy Walker, the whistleblower from Kaplan Industries in Florida. Over the years, we had become devoted friends, bonding over the abuses suffered by slaughter-bound animals. Tim had been an emotional support to me through my cancer battle. Now, when I disclosed my visual problems, he patiently listened and always made a point of offering to share his modest home in Naples with me, should I need a respite. It was strictly a platonic friendship, and a generous offer.

When we spoke, we would discuss politics (we'd agreed to disagree), our lives in Florida and Montana, his early experiences as a Navy sailor, the mundane things friends talk about. Sometimes, I would take the phone outside so he could hear the sound of the lake waves crashing on the shoreline in my front yard. He would bring me up to date on his new position as a USDA investigator, and I would keep him apprised of the slaughter violations I was somehow continuing to document.

Tim was not totally surprised by my revelations. After all, he would often remind me that, when he initially complained to supervisors about the fact that live cows were having their heads skinned, "They told me that the problems I described existed all over the country," he said. "That they were just a little worse at Kaplan's." Little could we have known that violations far *worse* than those at Kaplan's existed all over the country.

118

Giving Voice to the Voiceless 119

And Tim and I would reminisce about our work together.

"Remember the time you hung out at that sketchy, low-income project trying to find the Kaplan knocker?" Tim asked. That was when I had been searching for plant witnesses to corroborate Walker's claims. Visiting that rundown neighborhood had been nothing to me, just par for the course as an investigator. But for some reason, Tim had fixated on that incident. To him, it had been dangerous; I had exhibited courage. And he never let me forget it.

Invariably, our conversations would come around to the disposition of his whistleblower case. Tim had been deeply disappointed with the outcome; his frustration was palpable over the phone. Yes, he had testified before Congress on slaughter abuses. Yes, Kaplan Industries had been permanently shuttered. Yes, he had won back his USDA employment with retroactive pay and other concessions. And yes, I had written *Slaughterhouse,* exposing the abuses he had uncovered. He should have been delighted, right? Wrong.

This caring man desperately wanted his Kaplan Industries case to swing the door wide open to expose the much bigger issue of slaughter atrocities nationwide.

And finally, that's exactly what it did.

Chapter 34

For several years, I had been trying to convince a *Washington Post* investigative reporter to write a feature on slaughterhouse cruelty.

When I was in Washington, DC, to attend a meeting, I decided to drop by and pester journalist Joby Warrick again. As I walked down bustling L Street toward the newspaper's offices, it struck me: Warrick had previously won a Pulitzer Prize for a series on pig production that he had written for a newspaper in Raleigh, North Carolina.[1] Investigative reporter Duane Pohlman, who had exposed the IBP violations on Seattle TV, had earlier worked for a news station in Raleigh. I wondered what the chances were that they knew each other.

I met with Warrick and he seemed lukewarmly interested in the IBP scandal. When I got back to Montana, I telephoned Duane Pohlman, who did indeed know Warrick. A call from Pohlman to Warrick worked wonders.

Weeks later, I met up with Warrick in a motel room near Wallula, Washington, where he interviewed a number of IBP employees. I provided him with numerous documents and names of witnesses from other slaughterhouses I'd investigated across the United States. Warrick later conducted an in-depth interview with Tim Walker, as well.

Warrick and the *Washington Post*, one of the most influential papers in the world, published a groundbreaking feature, running three photos from our hidden camera footage showing a live cow dangling from the rail, on the front page of the newspaper, and revealing the industrywide atrocities I had documented. The *Post*'s independent analysis confirmed that cattle at slaughterhouses across the country were being skinned and dismembered while still fully conscious; hogs were being scalded alive. The title of the

Giving Voice to the Voiceless 121

article, taken from a quote by IBP's "second legger," was "They Die Piece by Piece."[2]

Washington Post readers—including some of the highest-ranking members of Congress—learned for the first time about the enormous suffering endured by slaughter-bound animals. The story ended up being one of the highest readership response pieces in the history of the *Washington Post*. Just as I suspected all along: if members of the public were simply given the information, they would show they care. My original strategy to document slaughterhouse violations across the country and then expose them through the media was working.

HFA then filed a petition for rulemaking with the USDA. We were again joined by the National Joint Council of Food Inspection Locals in submitting the petition to the USDA.

We announced our petition at a National Press Club news conference in Washington, DC, where USDA inspectors stepped forward to blow the whistle on their own agency. As they had in Washington State, the meat inspectors openly stated that, due to increased line speeds and industry deregulation, they could not enforce the Humane Methods of Slaughter Act.

The petition's request was simple: the USDA should permanently station inspectors in the areas of the plants where they could observe and monitor, on a full-time basis, live animals being slaughtered. HFA followed up with a full-page ad in the *New York Times* which referred to the USDA as the "U.S. Department of Atrocities" and urged people to write to the US agriculture secretary in support of the petition.

"Federal law is being ignored!" said Senator Robert Byrd, then serving as Senate president pro tempore, meaning he was third in line to the US presidency. He was so moved by the *Washington Post* story that he made an impassioned speech on the Senate floor. "Animal cruelty abounds. It is sickening. It is infuriating. Barbaric treatment of helpless, defenseless creatures must not be tolerated even if these animals are being raised for food—and even more so, more so. Such insensitivity is insidious and can spread and is dangerous. Life must be respected and dealt with humanely in a civilized society."[3] The senator's speech was heralded as a watershed event in the history of animal protection.

"USDA has the authority and capability to take action to reduce the disgusting cruelty about which I have spoken," Senator Byrd continued. Then, as chairman of the Senate Appropriations Committee, he secured funding to enforce the Humane Methods of Slaughter Act. While the HMSA had been enacted forty-three years earlier, this was the first funding ever allocated to enforce that law. When I heard the news, I was elated. I literally jumped up and down.

As it turns out, the USDA had, for the previous three years, completely stopped tracking the number of humane violations in slaughterhouses. For this reason, a resolution directing the USDA to enforce the law and reinstate tracking was introduced and ultimately inserted into the federal farm bill, which was approved by the full Congress and signed into law. Score one for the animals.

The investigative arm of Congress was then directed to examine the USDA's enforcement of the Humane Methods of Slaughter Act. Relying on the USDA's incomplete record-keeping, it revealed that systemic problems with enforcement were leading to the slaughter of "hundreds of thousands" of animals in violation of the law each year; that the "most prevalent non-compliance documented was the ineffective stunning of animals, in many cases resulting in a conscious animal reaching slaughter." The report concluded that, due to unreliable reporting and spotty enforcement, the USDA did not consistently document the scope and severity of violations. "The extent of noncompliance is likely to be greater than what is reflected [in records provided to investigators]."[4]

That's where renowned ethologist and conservationist Dr. Jane Goodall came in. While much of her work has focused on the study of chimpanzees in the wild, Dr. Goodall has great empathy for all animals, including those destined for slaughter.

A year after publication of the *Washington Post* story, at HFA's request, Dr. Goodall contacted Senator Byrd with information about the ways in which the USDA was misusing his funding and skirting compliance. After all, not a penny of the million dollars Senator Byrd had appropriated was being used to hire and station inspectors where they could monitor the slaughter process on a full-time basis. Instead, the money was used to hire seventeen veterinarians in district offices where they had no direct oversight over slaughter practices.

Surely, by now, I should have known better than to expect the USDA to do the right thing.

Prompted by his exchanges with Dr. Goodall, during a Congressional hearing, Senator Byrd put the US Secretary of Agriculture under President George W. Bush on the hot seat, asking basic questions about humane slaughter enforcement, which the secretary could not answer. Senator Byrd, unrelenting in his commitment to this issue, subsequently secured more money to hire inspectors to enforce the HMSA.

Since then, appropriations for the HMSA have increased somewhat, with Congress now funding roughly 148 "full-time equivalents" to enforce humane regulations. Full-time equivalents, in this case, are generally inspectors who make spot checks to observe humane handling and slaughter practices. Even with this increase in appropriations, today less than 3 percent of total funding for food safety inspection is devoted to humane handling and slaughter.[5] To the best of my knowledge, there are still no full-time inspectors stationed where they can *continuously monitor* the slaughter process specifically for humane violations at IBP/Tyson or at any of the country's nine hundred federally-inspected slaughterhouses.

Thanks to the USDA's fundamentally conflicted mission—*promoting* the sale of agricultural products while also *regulating* them—that agency has always been fixated on the former, increasing profits for agribusiness. With a crude revolving door in which meat industry leaders are appointed to the highest-ranking positions within the USDA, I doubt this will ever change.

Chapter 35

The walls of investigative reporter Duane Pohlman's Seattle office were plastered with prestigious awards he had won over the course of his career. Several Emmys were on display as well. Needless to say, Pohlman had proved himself to be an accomplished journalist.

And he was about to receive another honor: a Genesis Award for "Outstanding News Series" for his revealing TV exposés of conditions inside IBP.

The Genesis Awards, presented by The Ark Trust, an organization founded by the late Broadway actress Gretchen Wyler, were awarded to members of the media who had produced outstanding works that raised public awareness of animal issues. Past honorees had included Dr. Goodall, Anderson Cooper, Prince, David E. Kelley, Oprah Winfrey, and Sir Paul McCartney, as well as a long list of film and documentary producers and news reporters. The celebrity-packed gala was held annually in a ballroom at the posh Beverly Hilton in Beverly Hills, California.

Because Pohlman was among the honorees, I had scored a ticket and would be joining him at one of the elegantly set dinner tables in the Beverly Hilton ballroom. But before attending, I indulged myself with the Hollywood treatment, walking from the Hilton to a nearby Beverly Hills salon, where my hair was stylishly pulled back. After losing my tresses to chemo a few years earlier, my hair had grown back thicker and fuller than before. Having it professionally styled was indeed a luxury that wasn't lost on me. I returned to my room where I slipped into a black velvet dress with spaghetti straps, and made my way downstairs to the hotel lobby. I felt very glamorous.

It was thrilling to watch Duane walk the red carpet, and even more so when the master of ceremonies called Pohlman's name and he strutted up to the podium. Duane gave a compelling acceptance speech, talking about the plight of cattle at IBP. He then concluded his remarks by generously thanking me and asking me to stand. I, too, was given a round of applause. Blushing, I reticently soaked up the audience's appreciation.

This is all to say that because I was in Los Angeles for the Genesis Awards, and because the retina specialist at UCLA's Jules Stein Eye Institute had urged me to get my eyes tested annually, I had scheduled a second appointment for the following day at UCLA. I was as determined as ever to get to the bottom of my problem.

After all, it seemed that, back in Montana, I could no longer venture outside my little A-frame in daylight without my vision becoming grainy, which invariably triggered a migraine headache. I was now experiencing, on average, three such headaches a week. The chronic inflammation in my head was back.

A battery of tests was performed on me, including another electro-retinogram which revealed that my cone dystrophy was stable. It wasn't getting worse for now. Why, then, was I? Another test, called a fluorescein angiogram, was accomplished by injecting a chemical dye into the blood stream to photograph the blood vessels in the back of my eye. The chemical injection in my arm struck me as just a little too reminiscent of the chemotherapy drugs that had been pumped into me a few years earlier. After the angiography was performed, I found myself alone and sobbing in a bathroom stall of the spacious ladies' room on the first floor of the institute.

A year later, I would be invited back to the Genesis Awards to accept an award on behalf of the *Washington Post* for its story exposing violations at IBP. (*Post* reporters weren't permitted to accept such accolades, so I was sent in journalist Joby Warrick's place.) Before the ceremony, I would visit the same Beverly Hills hair salon, slip into the same spaghetti strap dress, and ultimately stand on the same podium where Duane Pohlman had made his acceptance speech. I would then address hundreds of attendees, offering gratitude and congratulations to the *Post*, and suggesting that other members of the press follow the newspaper's lead.

Once back at the graciously appointed dinner table, I leafed through the glossy Genesis Awards journal. I was stunned to find an "Open Letter to Gail Eisnitz," published as a full-page tribute in the spiral-bound journal.

"In 1989, I wrote to tell you that cows at the slaughterhouse where I was stationed were being skinned alive," began the letter. "Never could I have envisioned the rocky road we would travel as a result of that complaint—your thirteen-year struggle not only to uncover and document brutality in U.S. slaughterhouses, but also to expose those atrocities to American consumers. I am using the occasion of the Genesis Awards to publicly thank you." I could feel my face turning beet red.

The letter went on to list some of the obstacles I had faced, and concluded by saying, "I have spoken to you nearly every weekend for thirteen years. I've ridden the investigative rollercoaster and held your hand as the months turned into years. Whatever anyone reads in the newspaper, sees on the television, or hears on the radio about the inhumane slaughter of animals is a direct result of your persistence and tenacity. You are a friend to millions of animals. You are a hero to me."

It was signed, "An ex-USDA whistleblower (Name withheld for obvious reasons)."

To say that I was profoundly touched would be an understatement. I knew immediately that this was another anonymous letter penned by Timothy Walker. It was anonymous because Tim was still employed by the USDA. His generous, public expression of what it had been to "ride that rollercoaster" with me was without a doubt one of the highlights of my career.

The glare I was experiencing now almost felt like a "white out." So, I used the occasion of my second Genesis trip to schedule yet another follow-up at UCLA.

That round of studies reiterated that I had "partial cone dystrophy, temporal optic atrophy" consistent with cone dystrophy, and "a moderate degree of macular dysfunction." While that was Greek to me, in the context

Giving Voice to the Voiceless 127

of what I was experiencing, it was cause for alarm. Was I doomed to a life of disorientation, migraine headaches, floaters, and glare? All I knew was that my condition was continuing to deteriorate, and no one was telling me what to do.

Part Five

By Sheer Power of Will

Chapter 36

It was a scene unlike anything I'd ever been a part of: a cold February afternoon, dozens of tribal members huddled together in their winter ski jackets, hands in pockets. There was the hereditary chief, an elder, of the Rosebud Sioux Tribe wearing his feathered warbonnet. Several tribal members were beating loudly on a large drum in a nearby circle. Standing next to me was animal activist and Indigenous advocate James Cromwell—also an Academy Award nominee widely known for his role as Farmer Hoggett in the movie *Babe*. Now, he was talking animatedly before reporters' cameras.

It was a news conference that we had scheduled in Rapid City, South Dakota, to shed light on a project that was slated to be the third-largest hog farm in the world, set to produce nearly *1 million pigs a year* on the nearby Rosebud Sioux Reservation, the second-poorest Indigenous reservation in the United States. We knew it would cause unconscionable suffering for both animals and workers at the thirteen proposed sites, consisting of 232 warehouse-like barns. We were also aware that it would generate roughly three times the amount of raw sewage produced by the entire human population of the state of South Dakota.

Because Indigenous lands are exempt from state environmental laws, and because there were limited job opportunities on the reservation—Rosebud had an 85 percent unemployment rate—a large agribusiness corporation had entered into a joint venture with the Rosebud Sioux Tribal Council. The corporation intended to use the remote, pristine tribal land—with its sweeping vistas dotted with prairie dog mounds—as a giant cesspool for its operation.

Since the federal government had not required adequate environmental studies before construction began on the immense facility, HFA was able to sue the corporation under US law.

We issued news releases, conducted press conferences, and did everything conceivable to educate tribal members about the impacts of factory farming on land, people, and animals. When tribal members became aware of the appalling conditions they had unwittingly invited into their community, they promptly ousted their tribal council, and voted in a new council that opposed the farm. The tribe realigned itself with HFA in the lawsuit—*against* the hog corporation. As the litigation proceeded, and as investors became jittery, construction on the hog factory ground to a halt after only 48 of the proposed 232 barns were built.

After two years of litigation, a federal court ruled in HFA's favor. Adding to our stunning victory was the fact that, by declining to hear the corporation's appeal, the US Supreme Court, in essence, upheld HFA's win. That was a decisive defeat for the hog corporation.

Once the significance of our victory sank in, I was delighted not only for our legal team, but for the millions of pigs who wouldn't be raised on that farm.

While HFA had succeeded in stopping the Rosebud project with the construction of only two out of the proposed thirteen sites—or 48 of the 232 barns—experience told me early on that, once up and running, those two sites would be rife with violations.

Chapter 37

HFA hired Bob Baker, my former HSUS coworker, to assist me on the Rosebud case. I'd known Bob—a tall, lanky man with brown hair, an engaging sense of humor, and a stellar track record—for many years, and realized that he would be a great asset to our investigation.

I had done some preliminary footwork and, now that the two sites were operational, I'd gotten leads about a couple of hog farm workers who were willing to talk with us. Bob and I flew to Sioux Falls, South Dakota, and made the three-hour drive out to the reservation in the south-central part of the state.

The first employee had served as a sheriff's deputy near the reservation, but had been offered a higher-paying job as a security guard at the hog farm. He talked with us for two hours, describing operating procedures, hazardous working conditions, and illegal activities inside the facility.

Next, a second worker shared with us a handful of graphic photographs he'd taken at the hog factory. They showed pigs with injured limbs and missing tails, bloated dead pigs in barn alleyways surrounded by live pigs, and a storage bin piled high with hundreds of pig carcasses.

After some discussion, and much to our surprise, the employee agreed to take a small video camera into the operation while at work. The footage we had obtained at the IBP slaughterhouse had been powerful evidence; it couldn't hurt to try to get videotape here.

About a week later, our videographer called to inform us that he had shot about forty-five minutes worth of tape.

Bob and I were haunted by the images we saw: animals limping across pens with volleyball-sized hernias dangling from their abdomens, others with large, infected abscesses on their legs. Coughing pigs. Pigs whose faces, ears, and hindquarters had been cannibalized by pen-mates, and others with blood-covered snouts from eating them. Pigs scooting on their rumps because they couldn't walk. Emaciated pigs. Dying animals trying to struggle to their feet. Dead piglets whose legs were trapped between floor slats. Piles and piles of dead, bloated, fly-covered pigs.

If we weren't going to reach people through their hearts, I thought, certainly, we would reach them through their stomachs.

From here on in, Bob was going to be the boots on the ground for this investigation. After all, I could barely work. Now, it seemed like the detail that I saw was more than my brain could process. It's hard to describe, except to say that visual input made my poor head feel like it was going to explode.

For a small fee, one tribal member agreed to drive around the nineteen hundred square mile reservation to make contact with current and former hog factory employees. The result: as winter approached, and with ten inches of snow on the ground, Bob traveled back to the reservation where a large group of workers—Indigenous, white, and African American—had gathered to speak with him. Bob audiotaped the conversation.

Bob explained that he'd come to the reservation in the hopes of improving conditions for both the employees and the animals at the hog factory. He then asked questions about health hazards associated with working at the facility. The workers discussed the chronic wheezing, shortness of breath, coughing up phlegm, and asthma that plagued them; the conjunctivitis and headaches they experienced while on site. Employees described the flurry of dust floating in the air like snowflakes and one woman said she'd miscarried from the overwhelming fumes. Because ammonia from the waste pits and dust particles from the feed built up to toxic levels, some workers said they vomited when they entered the barns.

There was also "hog rash"—causing uncontrollable itching and ultimately scarring—either from the high levels of feed particles in the air or

By Sheer Power of Will

from contaminants in the water which workers showered in before entering and exiting the operation.

Soon, the workers' complaints drifted to the pigs. The group said that, on a *good* day, there were only eighteen employees to care for all forty-eight thousand pigs at each of the two sites that had been constructed. That was fewer than one worker per barn, less than one employee to oversee two thousand animals. Not only that, there was also a high absenteeism rate, which rose dramatically on weekends and holidays. One employee said that out of eighteen workers at his site, sometimes only three or four would show up to work.

The consequence, the workers said, was that small, injured, and ill animals were either dragged from their pens into alleyways where they were provided no food or water, or were left among the general pig population to be attacked and killed by pen-mates.

"I don't know what it is," one worker explained, "but pigs get pulled out of their pens and put in the alley and just forgotten about. You see a lot of them, they're just pulled out and they'll die for whatever reason. They usually starve out."

"They'll lay out there three, four, five days," said another. "Surprising how long a pig will go without eating. You walk that aisle and you can just step right over them and they won't even move."

The animals were in such crowded quarters, said another, that if one went down, employees would not be able to find it. It would be consumed by more dominant pigs by the time morning rolled around. The workers had coined a nickname for the animals' remains; they called them "rugs." A rug, explained an employee, resembled a bear rug that one might see in somebody's home. "It's a pig whose ribs have actually come apart and it's basically flat except for the head."

Animal scientists have established that cannibalism among pigs is caused by barren, impoverished surroundings. This means overcrowding, competition for food, lack of stimulation, and inadequate ventilation.[1]

When it came to killing smaller pigs who were sick, injured, or simply didn't grow fast enough, employees were expected to use a process called "thumping." That's where workers grab the pigs by their hind legs and smash them headfirst into the concrete floor. A lot of times, the pigs wouldn't die on the first few hits. Either way, "People just figure they throw them in the dead box and they'll freeze to death or what not," said a worker.*

As for disabled pigs that were too big to thump, "People take that straight hammer and just start wailing on them," explained another employee. "Hit them in the head three or four times." When pigs were deposited in alleyways and unable to move, he'd "watched four or five people take turns standing on their necks to suffocate them."

"The way to do it now," added another worker, "is we take the water hose and stick it down their throat and blow them up, and their buttholes pop out." That was the sure way to kill them, he said. "I mean, that's just the easy way to do it."

The videotape the worker had shot for us had depicted dozens of listless and dead piglets littering the "nursery" floor. These poor animals had fallen into the open spaces between floor slats—too big for their little feet to negotiate. Unable to extricate themselves because their entrapped legs would swell, the piglets were simply abandoned to starve. Others spent the overnight hours wedged in the floor under brooder heat lamps; workers who could smell their bodies burning the next morning had dubbed them "baby back ribs," "crispy critters," and "dead bacons."

Not only were the animals dead, but the workers' hearts were, too. It was distressing, but familiar, to me to see how the employees, forced to commit abuses, had become so inured to the piglets' suffering that they made jokes about it.

And sanitation was a serious problem. Waste pits under the pens were seldom flushed and manure hardened and built up, causing "shit clogs" impervious to the surge of flushing water. "Rugs" clogged drainage pipes and sewage water would flood up and over the slatted flooring. Piglets could

---

* Some producers gas smaller pigs with CO_2, another practice that has serious welfare implications.

be seen swimming in the waste, their heads sticking up, and larger pigs, sloshing around in sewage, became caked with manure. Contaminated flush water would engulf feed trays and water nipples. With no access to food and water, sometimes for days, animals resorted to eating manure and drinking urine from cesspools.

When employees power-washed empty barns, they would be splashed with waste water and other filth. The workers, still clad in their dirty uniforms, would then tend to issues in other barns. "You're carrying all that shit that's on you," explained one swinesman, "and all the germs that these other pigs died from, and you're spreading the sickness to the other pigs."

The hostile conditions the workers described all contributed to exceedingly high pig mortality rates. While the target death rate at the time the pigs reached slaughter weight was supposed to be 5 percent, some barns recorded mortality rates as high as 50 to 60 percent. "That was more than half the barn that died in six months," another worker shared.

"The worst barn we had up there," said one woman, "there were probably between three hundred and five hundred pigs left alive in the barn and the rest just died. Out of about eighteen hundred."

I wondered how the corporation could sustain such losses and stay financially afloat. If producers didn't care for their animals out of a basic sense of decency, surely, they would do so to protect their bottom line. Wrong. In any event, the "dead truck" collected the pigs' lifeless carcasses on its daily rounds, and off to the rendering plant they went to be turned into components of cement, crayons, and cosmetics, to name just a few of the many products which contain rendered hogs.

Chapter 38

Over the next several weeks, we would obtain even more videotape of shocking conditions inside the operation. Based on the group discussion and a number of individual interviews Bob had conducted, we planned to draft a tidy complaint to submit to the county prosecutor.

First, however, I tracked down a *New York Times* reporter who had weeks earlier written a story about contaminated meat at a Midwestern slaughterhouse. After I described conditions at the hog factory, she agreed to write an exposé. Bob traveled back to the reservation to introduce the reporter to several of the workers he had met. While I, with the help of a transcriptionist, furiously transcribed tapes from the interviews Bob had conducted.

In total, we had eight hundred pages of graphic testimony—with information even more disturbing than what is in this book—describing egregious violations at the hog farm. From that, we prepared the complaint that included a legal analysis of state laws being violated, key excerpts from workers' statements, as well as appalling photographs.

The county prosecutor declined to take the case, so HFA submitted the complaint, along with the mountain of testimony, contact information (with workers' permission), videotape, and photographs, to the South Dakota attorney general, the top law enforcement official in that state. The next day, *The New York Times* ran its scathing story, entitled "Indians Now Disdain a Farm Once Hailed for Giving Tribe Jobs, Treatment of Hogs and Workers is Issue in South Dakota."[1]

Six long weeks passed before the attorney general conducted a so-called investigation at the hog factory. Instead of executing a search warrant, the State waited to schedule a visit until it had received a formal invitation from farm officials to tour the facilities. According to employees, prior to the visit, management instructed workers to drag sick and dying pigs out of their pens and kill debilitated pigs that had been left to die in alleyways. Pigs were shifted from one barn to another to reduce overcrowding, and truckloads of diseased animals were shipped offsite.

None of the eyewitnesses was ever contacted by the AG's office. Nor was HFA.

Six months later, as violations persisted at the operation and workers documented them with yet even *more* videotape, HFA ran advertisements throughout the state urging the attorney general to conduct a more thorough investigation. At the top of the advertisement appeared a photo of a pig. Under the photo read the headline:

WHAT'S MISSING FROM THIS PICTURE?

"His ears," read the copy. "Due to the hostile living conditions at the factory farm where he's being raised, this young pig has just had his ears eaten off by stronger pigs. If that's all that happens to him, he'll be lucky. More likely, the other pigs will next go after his tail and ultimately eat him alive. All that will be left will be his hide and bones." Also featured were pictures of a pig being devoured alive, a seriously injured pig left to die in an alleyway, and two pigs with abdominal ruptures the size of volleyballs. Thanks to a mailing sent to HFA's quarter-million members, the AG's Office was flooded with postcards.

Another six months passed without further action. HFA provided the State with new evidence documenting additional violations and ran more advertisements statewide.

Again, instead of taking action, the Attorney General staunchly defended the factory hog corporation to the press, saying, "A mortality of two percent or three percent can be expected. . . . There's no business incentive for any hog operation to abuse their critters. They gain weight because they're happy and contented. . . . The suggestion that these folks were systematically abusing their critters flies in the face of good business practices."[2]

Long story short, responding to HFA's hard-hitting ads, the attorney general then mailed a five-page letter to thousands of concerned citizens, essentially ignoring all evidence. Taking his lead from the Washington State/IBP playbook, he spent the bulk of his letter attacking HFA, its motives, and its advertisements, and defending the hog factory's corporate management.

In his letter, the attorney general used bold typeface to quote the swine specialist who had been present during the State's announced "investigation":

I find this site to be managed at a level comparable to the top twenty-five percent of the operations in South Dakota. I found no evidence of animal abuse nor any evidence to support the other claims made against this operation. I believe it to be a well-run and managed operation and the manager and employees need to be commended for their efforts.

No charges were ever filed.

Shortly thereafter, the governor appointed the attorney general to the position of South Dakota circuit court judge.

On a brighter note, the hog corporation found it unsustainable to operate only two of the proposed thirteen sites, most particularly under the harsh, hostile conditions we had documented, and the factory farm eventually ceased operations.

Chapter 39

The media called him the "poet laureate of contemporary medicine"[1] and "one of the great clinical writers of the twentieth century."[2] Dr. Oliver Sacks was indeed the most celebrated neurologist in the world. He had published hundreds of scientific articles, and was widely known for his many best-selling books—collections of case studies of people and how they coped with strange neurological disorders. *Awakenings*, a 1990 Oscar-nominated movie starring Robin Williams and Robert DeNiro about patients suffering from encephalopathy who were temporarily brought out of their catatonic state, had been adapted from Sacks's memoir of the same name. I knew that another of his books, entitled *An Anthropologist on Mars*, was based in part on the life of Dr. Temple Grandin, the well-known autistic professor and humane slaughter consultant whom I had reached out to on my slaughterhouse cases.

I had dropped quite a bit of weight from an already slender physique. Desperate, experiencing three migraines a week, frightened by the extreme glare I was seeing, my brain feeling like it was going to explode from too much detail, and now, experiencing a constant hissing sound in my ears, I phoned Temple Grandin for Dr. Sack's contact information, which she readily gave me.

I wrote him a letter.

Dear Dr. Sacks,
I am hoping that you will be able to add a piece to a puzzle that I have been trying to solve for nearly thirty years. I am a colleague of Temple Grandin's and I have written this letter to you in my head

many times over the last ten years. Interestingly, Temple and I both work in the same area of animal protection.

In a nutshell:

1. I am a red-green colorblind woman, age forty-five.
2. Beginning at about age six, I have suffered from OCD.
3. Since menopause (age thirty-five—from chemotherapy), I have suffered very frequent migraines with no apparent visual symptoms. Family members have histories of ophthalmic migraines.
4. I've had an unusual visual/perceptual "flooding" problem since my early teens that sometimes makes the most ordinary tasks extremely frightening and difficult. I often see much more information than my brain seems to be able to process. When my brain gets "overloaded," I become spatially disoriented, my depth perception becomes impaired, and I lose sense of perceptual focus.
5. I have an apparent retinal problem. I now have extreme glare and floaters that are so disruptive that I seldom participate in outdoor activities anymore. Migraines are also triggered by outdoor activities.
6. As a child, I used to describe the world as being made up of "dots." In recent years, my vision has become increasingly pixelated.

I have had MRIs, EEGs, VERs, ERPs, and ERGs. I've worn color-blind contact lenses. I occasionally wear yellow tinted lenses to reduce glare. I attended "visual training" classes twice a week for two years. I've been told that I have everything from frontal lobe epilepsy to PTSD to cone dystrophy. Neurologists at UCLA claim that I may be "in a constant state of migraine."

An interesting tidbit: Despite the color deficiency, I entered the animal protection field as a self-taught wildlife illustrator. As one art critic once wrote, I "made up for the lack of color in my work by attention to detail." I attribute this to the way I see the world in a pixelated fashion.

I assume that the retinal issue—whatever it may be—may be partially responsible for my problems. I also grant that there may be a psychological component. However, I believe that migraine plays a part as well.

Dr. Sacks, I would be very grateful to you for any possible light that you may be able to shed on the usual perceptual symptoms I have described, as I have become somewhat desperate.

Dr. Sacks's office responded to my letter and an appointment was scheduled. The doctor was practicing at New York University Medical Center, so I made the long trip from Montana. My brother-in law, Bob, kindly accompanied me by bus into the city. I took off my oversized sunglasses and sat in the waiting room anticipating my appointment with Dr. Sacks.

The doctor was in his late sixties, had a distinguished British accent and a white beard. None of that was a surprise to me, as I had seen him interviewed many times on television. In fact, just that morning, as we were preparing to leave to catch the bus, I happened to see him on a network morning show talking about his latest neurological project.

The doctor's examination was comprehensive. He performed the typical neurological tests for physical reflexes—tapping on my knees with a small mallet and also asking me to track his finger with my gaze—and conducted an in-depth personal history. He then asked me to wait outside his office door, and he spoke to Bob for at least fifteen minutes. What were they talking about? What was it that he couldn't say to my face? I stood outside his office, despairing, tears streaming down my face.

Weeks after my visit, I obtained a copy of Dr. Sacks's seven-page hand-typed report. I was most interested in his conclusions.

"Not easy to put all this together," he wrote, "—or does it all belong together. I am not sure whether the retinal pathology could go with her 'pixelation.' Most of her other visual symptoms would go with a migraine-equivalent continuum of cortical sensitivity and, as such, might be helped with Neurontin—a drug with wide uses in a variety of hyperexcitable syndromes.

"The 'overwhelming' is puzzling—I do not know what to make of it, though I have heard similar descriptions from many people with some autistic traits, and this may be the case with Ms. Eisnitz too.

"Despite these overwhelming sounding symptoms," he continued, "Ms. Eisnitz will often, by sheer power of will, continue writing or working going through her attacks and not 'capitulating' to them."

He concluded his remarks by saying, "I also cannot help thinking that her isolated life in Montana has finally become intolerable, and that a change of venue, a change of life, may be a prerequisite to real improvement." Truer words were never written.

"I do hope that this gifted, brave, but now rather tormented woman, with so much capacity to give and receive, can be helped to a healthier life. It is very moving to hear her brother-in-law say what a lively, life-loving person she was twenty years ago, and to contrast this with her painful state now."

I tried the Neurontin. It didn't work.

Chapter 40

I was, for the most part, largely nonfunctional, but, as Dr. Sacks had put it, I was operating now "by sheer power of will." I couldn't stop. Cases kept falling into my lap; I could not forsake the animals who were in such desperate need.

Joe Suing, a Rosebud Sioux tribal member who had read about the violations at the Rosebud hog factory in the newspaper, contacted HFA to provide information about conditions at the Nebraska farm where he worked. I phoned him and we had a lengthy discussion, during which time he explained that he was the only worker at the large confinement facility. Unlike Rosebud, which did not have a breeding operation on site, this particular farm was a complete pig production operation. It bred, "farrowed" (birthed), raised, and "finished" pigs until they reached market weight.

Suing was struggling to care for all two thousand animals on the premises. He desperately wanted to quit his job and return to work as a long-distance trucker, but he dreaded what would happen to the animals if he left the operation in the hands of a less conscientious replacement.

Female breeding pigs, called sows, at this facility—just like the majority of the 6 million other sows throughout the United States—were confined inside cages so small that they could not walk or even turn around. Provided no straw so that their dung could fall through to a waste pit below, the sows stood, ate, pooped, and slept on concrete slatted flooring which caused crippling arthritis and foot disorders. In addition, inhaling the noxious fumes from the waste pit below, they developed serious respiratory problems.

After about four months of immobilization in "gestation crates," the sows were loaded into another equally confining cage, called a "farrowing crate." There they gave birth and nursed their young on metal mesh

145

floors. Two weeks after birth, the newborns were taken from their mothers' sides. The sows were then returned to gestation crates and, within days, re-impregnated. This cycle of constant incarceration continued for years.

Because Suing worked essentially alone at the factory farm, he was able to shoot videotape of the operation. The images he sent me were even more disturbing than those at Rosebud. Here, pregnant sows, weighing between four hundred and six hundred pounds each, spent the bulk of their lives inside gestation crates that were only nineteen inches wide—even narrower than the standard industry width of twenty-two to twenty-four inches—and seven feet long.

Like sows on most factory farms, the animals had large open sores on their faces, shoulders, backs, legs, and hindquarters from constant contact with the crates' metal bars. Unable to perform the most basic and natural of behaviors—like walking, turning around, and nest building—these pitiful animals could be seen engaging in neurotic activities including head bobbing, rocking, and air chewing, behaviors similar to those exhibited by humans suffering from severe psychiatric disorders.

The video, shot with the assistance of a friend, depicted Joe, in his late forties and wearing green insulated coveralls, feeding the sows with a feed cart and scoop. Because there were no feed troughs inside the crates, he tossed the grain onto the concrete floor slats and, in some cases, onto the heads and backs of the sows. A lot of the feed fell into the waste pit below. Not surprisingly, without adequate feed, the animals appeared to be under-weight—"razor backed"—their spines were protruding under their skin. Joe had told me it was a struggle to get feed for the animals, despite the fact that the farm owner also operated a feed store.

I sent Joe's videotape to Dr. Peggy Larson, a veterinarian and friend with extensive experience in hog production. "The area with the gestation crates was nightmarish," she wrote after viewing the videotape. "I am aware of the different vocalizations of hogs. These hogs were making loud, long distressed sounds. Watching this video was akin to watching a torture film. Both the sound and the extreme immobilization of the sows in the crates were overwhelming to one's senses."

By Sheer Power of Will   147

I'd asked Bob Baker to visit Suing at the operation. When he arrived, Bob was so astonished at the sows' conditions—their coats were poor, they looked emaciated, wasted, one had a pile of fetuses behind her—that he immediately pulled his tiny video camera from his backpack and, with Joe's okay, started to shoot videotape.

In the farrowing rooms, flies swarmed around several buckets of dead piglets. There were holes in the wire mesh floors. Joe, looking down through the flooring, noticed a piglet silently swimming in the frigid waste pit. Bob chased the piglet down to Joe, who used a snare pole to catch it and place it under a heat lamp. Joe predicted it would soon die, which it did.

From the farrowing rooms, the two men ventured into the nurseries and grower and finisher barns. The growing and finishing pens were extremely crowded and the floors were encrusted with five-inch-deep excrement. Undersized pigs were in pens with normal sized pigs, and cannibalism was rampant. Sick pigs were humped up, coughing, and shivering. One appeared to have a broken leg; another was being trampled.

After Bob's visit, I conducted an even more extensive phone interview with Joe. I started by asking him about the piglet he and Bob had recovered from the waste pit. Finding piglets there, he said, wasn't an uncommon experience.

The previous Saturday, using his flashlight, Joe had discovered a number of piglets in the pit. "Once they fell in there, some of them were so far in the 'soup'," as Joe called the sewage, "that you could just see bubbles coming up through the manure. And I seen bubbles coming up and I knew something was in there. I could just barely see this one's snout crack through the manure, and I snared him. He didn't survive.

"There were a couple of pigs that were hanging on to the exhaust pipe for dear life," Joe continued, "and they were afraid to come up to the light. There were at least ten pigs that were still lying in there, drowned. There was no need to save them. I was just looking for bubbles."

Next, I nudged the conversation to the issue of pregnant sows. Joe explained that, now, in the dead of winter, there was no heat in the gestation room;

that the only heat generated came from the sows themselves. "The place is so drafty," he said, "and I'm sure there's cold air coming up [from the waste pit] through those cracks between the slats."

The water troughs in the crates had been flattened by the sows standing on them and, while the automatic waterers sent water flowing into the alleyways in front of some crates, other sows had no access to water at all.

"The trick question of the day," Joe said, "is, 'Will there be water or won't there be water?' There have been times when I took the water hose out and walked the hose down there and put it in their mouths. They would suck on that damn hose for ten minutes!"

And a lot of the sows were starving. "I'd imagine that if anyone came in here of high authority," Joe said, "out of the 150 sows that are in here, I'd say maybe that they'd destroy 75 of them on the spot."

As an example, Joe said that one downed sow lay in her gestation crate for close to a month. She couldn't eat or drink. He'd throw feed in the crate, and the feed just piled up on top of her head until it was about two inches thick. "The tears from her eye got covered up with feed. Her eye was encrusted until it finally rotted. All you could see was a wet pool where her eyeball was. When she died it was a pretty rotten mess.

"I took out two the other day—their whole hooves were missing," Joe said. "I don't know if they were caught under something. They had no hooves. Some of them lay in those crates so long their legs rot off."

The best an injured or dying sow could hope for was the rare occasion when she could be coaxed out of her crate alive, dragged outside, and shot. If he could just get her out of the crate and into the alleyway "with the little bit of power she has left," it was a big help. Much more often, however, downed sows simply died in their crates. "Basically, they just laid there until they died."

"How long would they lie there alive?" I asked.

"Weeks. Months. They probably should have been shot," he admitted. "But then again, you can't just go in there and kill everything that looks bad. Otherwise, there would be nothing left in there!"

By Sheer Power of Will 149

Injured and ill feeder pigs were left to suffer protracted deaths from infection, disease, dehydration, or starvation. A veterinarian had been to the operation once, Joe explained, but that was only because he had accidentally driven to the wrong farm.

Chapter 41

The odor knocks visitors off balance the moment they walk in the battered front door of HKY Farm. It's not so much a barnyard smell as a noxious combination of manure, ammonia, and death that intensifies as one moves toward the barns.

Next comes the sound of dozens of sows screaming and thrashing at their cages at the arrival of visitors and the prospect of food, a noise so loud and unsettling that a farm manager puts on ear plugs as he enters.

Inside, HKY Farm looks like a Third World prison for pigs....

—*Chicago Tribune*

So began a story I'd pitched to a journalist with the *Chicago Tribune*. The reporter and a photographer had traveled to Nebraska to meet up with Bob Baker and Joe Suing at the hog factory. Stunned by what he saw, the reporter wrote a compelling front-page story entitled "At Some Farms, It's 'Hog Hell': The Fumes, Diseased Animals in Manure Fouled Pens and Rotting Corpses Assault the Senses at a Facility in Nebraska. Critics Say It's Hardly Unique."[1]

It was, and is, hardly unique. Back in 1997—to my knowledge the only year for which *any* hog factory's mortality records were ever made public—an Oklahoma hog corporation was fined $88,000 for improper carcass disposal, due to dumpsters overflowing with pig corpses as well as decomposed skeletons littering the ground.[2] The state's water quality division alleged that the company's failure to dispose of carcasses in a timely manner increased the risk of disease spread and pollution of surface and ground waters.

The company cited its death losses in legal filings defending against the fine. That single corporation reported losses of 420,000 dead pigs—that was forty-eight pigs dying every hour, twenty-four hours a day for one full year.[3] These were not animals that were slaughtered, but pigs that died on the farm. These and millions of pigs across the United States died as a result of the hostile, disease-promoting conditions inside factory farms.

In addition to mortality from injury and illness, there are other catastrophic circumstances that result in heavy casualties. When electrical power, for instance, is lost from lightning strikes or any other cause, ventilation systems, sidewall curtains, and backup generators may fail and thousands of pigs can suffocate on the fumes of their own wastes in just a few short hours. Likewise, between 2015 and 2023, a spate of hog barn fires blasted through Canada, incinerating upwards of 105,000 live hogs[4]—some of them sows struggling to escape their gestation crates. Similarly, in the United States, since 2013, roughly 155,000 hogs have burned to death in barn fires.[5]*

Collecting pig eyeballs to test for the illegal drug clenbuterol, I once found myself at a rendering plant, standing knee-deep in animal carcasses. There, amidst the stench of decaying remains, with scalpel in hand, I excised eyeballs. Over the course of two days, I watched as dump trucks and tractor trailers, literally filled to the brim with dead pigs, arrived nonstop to unload their cargo—mountains of carcasses—into a pit with a giant auger—a small sampling of how many pigs expire on factory farms.

Bob and I worked around the clock preparing a comprehensive "Petition for Enforcement of Nebraska Animal Cruelty Statutes" at the facility. Aware that there were so many hog operations in that part of the state that it had

---

* Speaking of barn fires, it also bears mentioning that in 2023, the deadliest cattle barn fire ever recorded occurred at an operation in the Texas panhandle, killing a staggering 18,000 dairy cows. All totaled, according to the Animal Welfare Institute, since 2013, roughly 8.2 million animals—mostly chickens—have perished in barn fires in the United States.

been nicknamed "hog valley," and presuming again that the county prosecutor would not give serious consideration to the case, we filed the complaint with the Nebraska attorney general. In addition to providing Joe Suing's statement and expert opinions from large animal veterinarians, we included hours of videotape of conditions at the factory farm. "On its face," wrote HFA's Bradley Miller in the petition to the attorney general, "this evidence documents a pervasive pattern of abuse affecting thousands of animals. This blatant criminal activity merits immediate cessation and prosecution by your office."

Two weeks later we received word from the attorney general that he was bumping the matter down to the county prosecutor.

Two long months passed without any action. Bob and I were so frustrated that we asked HFA's lawyer to send a strongly worded letter to the attorney general, demanding again that immediate and decisive action be taken. Shortly thereafter, we learned from the attorney general's office that the owner of the hog factory, facing the possibility of being criminally charged, opted to shut the facility's doors for good. It was a circuitous route to accomplish our goal, but it was a win for the animals, nonetheless.

Chapter 42

"This is a forty-seven-year-old female referred for neuro-ophthalmologic evaluation," wrote a Montana doctor. "The patient reports that her primary eye problems relate to glare, photosensitivity, numerous bilateral floaters, difficulty with night vision, and 'visual overload.' She says that she has seen the world as 'pixelated' since early childhood.

"There has been a question of temporal lobe epilepsy in the past and she has been treated with anti-seizure medication, and another EEG showed subtle abnormality suggestive of 'chronic migrainosus.' This was unsuccessfully treated with high-dose steroids.

"No treatable eye condition has been identified."

At my urging, my mom, then seventy-two years old, took twelve hours' worth of connecting flights from my parents' home in Asheville, North Carolina, all the way to the northwest corner of Montana. After all, her child was in the middle of nowhere and was losing it.

I'd put my mother, father, sister, and brother-in-law through the wringer for years with my complaints about this condition. They'd tried to support me in every way they could. Suddenly, it felt like there was an unspoken contract within my family to not "enable" Gail. I'd visited so many doctors; I sensed that my family concluded that I must be experiencing psychological problems.

During her visit to Montana, my mom proved me right.

One evening, as I lay gripped with fear in bed in the sleeping loft of my A-frame, my mother climbed the stairs to speak with me. After so many years of listening to my woes, trying to help me, and feeling utterly powerless to relieve my distress, Mom, a compassionate and doting woman, suddenly sought to convince me that my mental health was at stake.

"You're sick!" she exclaimed in frustration, looking me square in the eye and pointing a finger at me. "You're sick!" she repeated, obviously feeling helpless to fix me. She was no longer in my camp, she no longer thought that my underlying issue was eye-related; she believed it was in my head. But I had already visited a number of psychology and psychiatry professionals, to no avail. Her accusation cut deeply and left me reeling from the blow.

There was not a lot Mom could do for me, anyway. She did encourage me to fly back to Asheville with her where my family would, once and for all, take me to Duke University Medical Center in Durham, North Carolina. I had already been to so many teaching hospitals. What was the point? I resisted and, after a week, my mother, feeling incapable of helping me, boarded a plane for the lengthy flight home.

Again, like the terrified polar bear cubs on the PBS documentary that I'd watched as teen, I was fraught with feelings of fear and abandonment. Alone in the world with my visual problem again, there was nowhere left to turn; I was on my own.

Several months later, I capitulated and made the trip to Asheville. It would turn into a four-month odyssey I would not soon forget.

The sun looked like a nuclear explosion. My eyes were swollen and burning and I was experiencing migraines with increased frequency. My ears were ringing loudly. The glare hurt, my vision shimmered, my brain was overloaded.

"She flew in from Montana to stay with her parents and comes to the ER for evaluation," wrote the emergency room doctor at Asheville's hospital. "She says she is having a nervous breakdown and is suicidal for the first time. She is not hallucinating or seeing things that are not there. She has not been this way before. She is not homicidal. She thinks this visual problem is making her psychologically unstable. She says she goes outside during the day and has to wear dark glasses because she gets too much information visually.

By Sheer Power of Will

She gets a lot of floaters, shimmering, and she has a hard time having her eyes adjust to night vision."

The doctors in the ER admitted me to the hospital psych ward for a three-day stay.

My parents and sister were convinced that Duke University Medical Center in Durham was the gold standard. It did have a stellar reputation, but so did many of the institutions I'd already visited. Dad, Mom, and I made the four-hour drive from Asheville, and my sister, Lisa, flew in from Pennsylvania.

The next morning—while Dad stayed back at the hotel—we found ourselves in the neuro-ophthalmology clinic's small waiting area, my pupils dilating, Mom and Lisa seated next to me, our backs to the wall. No one spoke a word.

When the time came for the exam, the neuro-ophthalmologist used a bright light to look through my dilated pupils at my optic nerves. Everything checked out, he said.

Next, I saw an endocrinologist. Aware that my hormones were dysregulated—a long-term consequence of chemotherapy—I wanted to see if they could be the cause of a confused brain. I knew it was a long shot, but I was desperate. We saw the doctor; her nurse drew a blood sample for analysis, and that was that. I had scheduled one final appointment with yet another retina specialist for the following day.

Mom, Lisa, and I were leaving the endocrinology department's waiting area when Lisa unexpectedly walked away to make a phone call to arrange for her flight back to Pennsylvania. She returned to the waiting area and said she had booked the next available flight home that evening.

I hadn't been able to see straight for decades. I lived in a dreamlike state, in a world of confusion. In recent years, the visual detail had become so overwhelming that it felt like my brain was going to crack into pieces. With no resolution to this enduring problem, and no closer to a diagnosis, I felt like my big sister was throwing in the towel. Here she had put her busy lawyer schedule on hold, flown all the way down to North Carolina to accompany me to these appointments, and yet, the fearful child in me thought she was deserting me—leaving me to be dependent on my aging parents.

All of a sudden, out of nowhere, a wave of rage overtook me. "Fuck you!" I said, glaring at my sister. "Fuck you!" I repeated. I had an all-too-vivid vision of strangling her. Short of strangling my sister, I tossed my handbag at her and stormed off down the medical center's wide, tiled hallway, disappearing from my family's sight. It hadn't been much of a spectacle, but, since I was usually mild mannered, it was the biggest confrontation of my life.

I stopped by a large window in an atrium, stood there, dumbstruck, and looked down at the manicured medical center grounds below. Again, I didn't know what to do or where to turn. I'd survived cancer, and yet, this visual problem seemed easily to be a thousand times more insurmountable. How was I going to function? How was I going to do my job? Pay my rent? Would I end up living with my parents, dependent on them?

Stunned, I stared out the window for ten long minutes, drowning in my own helplessness. Then, like a zombie, I collected myself and walked back to the waiting area where my mom and sister stood. With them was a uniformed university security guard. He directed us to the medical center's tram.

"You do know where we're going," my mom assertively said to me, as the tram doors opened automatically. We were headed to the emergency room, where I was to be put in lockdown. Like an automaton, I just followed along.

The little chamber was in the bowels of Duke's emergency room. The seating area was shiny and rigid and appeared to be molded into the floor like a giant lump of clay. There was nothing movable and nothing removable. It was more a prison cell than anything else; perhaps a rubber room? For crazy people like me?

There was a large clock in an alcove across from my tiny prison. I watched as the second hand slowly ticked by. I saw sick people being wheeled in on gurneys by patient transport, stopping briefly at the alcove, and I could hear their complaints: a woman who was having an asthma flare, a man who had suffered a heart attack.

By Sheer Power of Will 157

I was jealous of that man with the heart attack. *I wanted to be him.* I wanted to have a "real" problem, a diagnosable condition; to know what was wrong with me; even if it was a heart attack. I was *that* desperate to end the madness.

Like an injured sow in a gestation crate, clueless about her confinement, defeated, I didn't know why I was there. I hadn't done anything terrible. I waited, waited, alone with my confusion and fears, for something, anything, to happen. But nothing did.

Sitting alone on the hard surface, I watched the hands move ever more slowly around that clock. Three interminable hours later, my mother, sister, and a medical center social worker entered the little room. They sat down across from me on the glossy molded seating on the other side of the cell.

"Gail, why do you think you're here today?" the social worker asked.

I tried to calmly explain why I was so upset, why I had lashed out, and how I couldn't see or think straight. But the social worker was having none of it.

Neither were my loved ones.

Not sure why, but eventually I was "released" from detention, and we three made our way back—first on the tram, then down a series of escalators—to the car, and eventually to the hotel. There was small talk, but little was said.

My sister did not travel home that evening; she scheduled a flight for the next morning. I did not join my family for a late dinner at a nearby Mexican restaurant. Instead, I sat on the hotel room bed—in total darkness, to sooth my sore eyes, my weary brain—hands to my face, sobbing uncontrollably. What was to become of me? I wept so hard that my eyes felt caustic, I believed they were going to ignite.

Chapter 43

Years earlier, a doctor at the Mayo Clinic had suggested that I might be suffering from, among other things, "somatization." Somatization, as I mentioned before, is the process whereby unexpressed stress and emotions manifest in the body as physical symptoms. Because no doctor before or since Mayo had been able to identify the source of my very real symptoms, I got it in my head that perhaps suppressed emotions could be at the root of my problem.

After all, I'm not very fluent in the language of emotions—particularly grief and loss. As a child, I connected on a profound level with animals. But, as I began documenting violations, to protect my heart, I shut down. For me, it became safer to not feel.

Yes, I had cried a year earlier at neurologist Oliver Sacks's office; I had sobbed in the hotel room near Duke. Those were tears of sheer frustration. But, no, I had never wept for all the animal suffering I had documented and exposed. No tears for the millions of animals being skinned, dismembered, or scalded alive, thumped, or confined in crates. Not one single tear.

I was desperate to get in touch with any suppressed emotions that might be causing my problems, but the recovery centers I'd researched—where therapists help patients focus on past trauma—were cost prohibitive: $29,000 for a seven-week stay. My insurance didn't cover this, and I didn't have that kind of dough.

Over the course of six years in Montana, I had made a couple of good friends who had seen me go from a bubbly, enthusiastic, highly functioning member of society to a mere shadow of myself—literally and figuratively wasting away before their very eyes. Worried about my well-being, my friend Marc footed the exorbitant bill. Now *that's* a good friend.

I flew from Asheville to an airport in the high desert of the southwestern United States. Picked up at baggage claim by a man who was driving a generic white van, I was transported another sixty miles to the recovery center. The promotional materials I had received about the facility advertised it as a behavioral health, trauma, and addiction treatment center. The colorful brochure had pictures of a labyrinth for walking meditation, a small cottage—which I had assumed was one of the sleeping quarters—and the vibrant multicolored scenery of the setting desert sun. On the phone, the sales staff had assured me that this was the perfect place for me to exorcise my demons. I was filled with hope.

After the nine-hour journey to the facility, I was exhausted. Hope flew out the window when the van driver steered the vehicle down a dusty dirt road and dropped me off at a shabby, unwelcoming trailer. Inside the dingy structure, an intake coordinator handed me a small plastic cup and instructed me to go into the tiny bathroom and provide a urine sample. For someone who had spent a lifetime suppressing her feelings, I was surprised to be hit with a wave of panic and distress. Tears welled up in my eyes. What had I gotten myself into? Had my selection of this facility been a huge mistake?

In my mind's eye, I had pictured the treatment center's main building as a professional looking, spacious facility. I couldn't have been more wrong. What I had assumed from the promotional photos was a small cottage for a handful of residents turned out to be the operation's main hub. That's where the bulk of activities—individual, group, and art therapy, workshops, and yoga—took place, where "residents" themselves, assigned in shifts, prepared food and washed dishes, and congregated for meals.

Tears ran down my cheeks as I was shown to my bedroom. From the outside, the accommodations resembled a series of Wild West cabins strung together like a seedy motel. At the end was a medication shack where residents lined up to have their pills dispensed. From the inside, the bedroom, which housed three people, was adequate—three twin beds, three desks, and three chairs. I would have only one roommate at first, an alcoholic whose father had put a gun to her head.

The first day of "treatment," I would meet with Anna, a psychologist in her fifties who wore a pantsuit and low heels. Her initial order of business was to complete, with my input, a written treatment plan for my "recovery." In flowery script, she wrote down my problems, objectives, and the center's guaranteed results. "Not being heard or acknowledged, lack of sense of self," she jotted down as two presenting problems, "OCD, physical/somatic problems like vision and migraine." She then boldly wrote on the intake form, that, at the conclusion of the seven-week program, "Client will have a decrease in negative or critical self-statements; an increase in self-trust and self-identity; and will be able to experience feelings more directly and spontaneously." At the rate of $170 per therapy session, she was apparently going to work magic on me.

Next, I visited with a poker-faced psychiatrist who prescribed me a cocktail of psych drugs.

In the days ahead, I would participate in a number of programs. In group therapy, we were instructed to draw a timeline on a large sheet of sketch paper to chronologically chart our life's traumas. Once completed, we individually presented our timelines to the six-member group. After sharing my timeline, I was coached by the therapist to lie on a blanket that she had spread out on the carpeted floor. She then knelt down and wrapped me up tightly, swaddling me like a baby, in what was supposed to be a cathartic exercise for me. It wasn't.

Another strategy for awakening repressed emotions: In a large room with a durable laminate floor, a group of us was instructed to get down on our hands and knees, make a fist, and start pounding on the floor with all our might, vocalizing as we whacked. When emotions are not readily accessible, I speak from experience that banging on a rock-hard surface is going to do little more than really hurt one's hand.

And yes, I was highly self-critical, didn't have a sense of who I was, nor did I think I was worthy of love. At this treatment center, I was told to repeat a host of positive affirmations—"I am lovable . . . I am a worthwhile human being . . . I am worthy of love from myself and others"—as if, after decades

By Sheer Power of Will 161

developing self-destructive behaviors, reciting these empty statements would miraculously cure my ills.

In time, it became abundantly clear that I had checked myself into what was an aftercare program for people with chemical dependency. In other words, individuals who had spent at least a month in treatment at facilities like the Betty Ford Center subsequently booked a stay at this operation to reduce their chances of relapse. In short, it was an expensive babysitting service for recovering addicts.

Amazingly, there was one silver lining in this whole disastrous experience which led me to believe that maybe I was right where I was supposed to be.

Every Saturday morning, the entire group of thirty residents would crowd together in the little cottage to hear one patient tell his or her dramatic life story. As chance would have it, or something bigger than chance, over the course of two Saturdays, two residents shared scandalous and lurid accounts of life growing up with their abusive families in their affluent homes. Both stories focused entirely on the brazen debauchery that their fathers had engaged in. The twisted and perverse descriptions were more debased than any human tale I had ever heard. As life would have it, it turned out that the fathers they spoke about were both chief executives of two of the largest and most prominent slaughterhouse companies in the United States.

What were the odds?

One morning, six weeks into what was to be a seven week stay, I was to rise at 7:45 a.m., shower, walk to the little cottage for breakfast and then to 9 a.m. "group therapy." But by eight o'clock, I was still under the covers and did not want to get out of bed.

After about forty-five minutes, I pulled the blankets off. At that moment, I realized this addiction rehab babysitting service had done nothing to help me and was only making me worse. I made the decision to leave the facility, packing my bags, shuttling to the airport, and catching the next Montana-bound flight home.

And so, I returned to Montana, back where I had started, with absolutely nothing to show for my four-month odyssey. The bane of my travel had been how terribly I had missed my beloved tabby cat, Bobby Rae. I was shell shocked when I arrived home, and even more so to find that my little A-frame had been trashed by my pet sitter. I'd been in touch with her often during my sojourn and thankfully, Bobby Rae was okay. But she had destroyed personal property and littered the house with so many cigarette butts that I was grateful she hadn't burned the place down.

After cleaning up, I started packing up. I had no choice but to move east to Asheville where I would have my parents' support. With the help of a second friend, Val, I boxed up my household possessions and office items and arranged for a moving company to transport my belongings—my car included. Bobby Rae and I made the twelve-hour flight to Asheville. I felt dazed and defeated.

My parents had rented an apartment for me in Asheville. The months which followed would take me to new depths—a new low—too low for me to even put into words.

Part Six

No Milk of Human Kindness

Chapter 44

HFA had received a tip about a sprawling dairy farm complex in the Pacific Northwest, housing scores of thousands of cows, heifers, and calves and producing well over a hundred thousand gallons of milk a day. According to the United Farm Workers (UFW), the nation's largest farm workers' union, farm employees there had previously claimed that they had been required to use two-by-fours to beat unwanted male calves to death. The practice had reportedly made the local news.

The overwhelming majority of dairy cows today live on factory farms. Some cows are intensively confined in large barns where they are tethered by the neck in "tie stalls." Others, those in "free stall" operations, only have access to alleyways and small sleeping areas called "beds." Separated by metal bars, the beds are just wide enough to accommodate each cow. In most free stall mega-dairies, there are fewer beds than cows, preventing all cows from lying down at once. That's a problem, because cows in such operations would normally lie down about ten to twelve hours a day.

Other cows live outside on "dry lots." A dry lot is a dirt enclosure with no vegetation, depriving animals of the opportunity to graze as they normally would for at least six hours a day. Cows are provided little, if any, shelter and, in inclement weather, dry lots can quickly turn into killing fields. In cold temperatures, cows may freeze to death; in hot weather, they may suffer from lack of shade and die of heat stress; in wet weather, they become mired in muck, a combination of their waste and mud.

To keep cows on dairy farms producing milk ten months a year, they are kept pregnant and/or producing milk the entire time they are at the operation.

At some large dairies, lactating cows are herded to the milking parlor, where they are loaded, for automatic milking, onto large elevated revolving platforms called "carousels." Workers quickly hook cows up to milking machine suction cups. After approximately eight minutes, the cows have made a complete revolution around the carousel and have been fully milked. Each carousel allows for thousands of cows to be milked twice a day.

While cows would normally produce less than two gallons of milk a day to supply their calves' needs, cows today produce on average six to seven gallons of milk per day. In peak periods, they can generate almost twice the amount. This enormous jump in production has been accomplished through changes in nutrition, milking procedures, genetic manipulation, and the use of antibiotics and hormones.

This increase in milk production takes a toll on the cows as their bodies are pushed metabolically beyond their limits. The consequence is that cows are removed from the dairy herd (or "culled") and shipped to slaughter at three to five years of age. That's compared to their natural life span of roughly twenty years.

Cows inside factory farms, like pigs, don't adjust well to life on concrete slabs. Forced to stand in feces and urine, which damage their hooves and cause them to slip and fall, cows often become lame. Huge bloated udders, due to the artificially large production of milk, cause an unnatural gait. Lameness and injury are the leading causes of death in dairy cows. Mastitis, on the other hand, is a very painful and potentially fatal inflammation of the udder caused by overmilking, hormone administration, unsanitary conditions at the time of milking, and filthy living environments. At factory farms, mastitis, fertility issues, and lameness are the most common reasons for culling.

As for their offspring, female calves are generally raised to replace the current milking herd. They are housed in total isolation in tiny hutches. Male calves, worthless for milk production, are a surplus product of the dairy industry. They are often transported to auction where some are sold as babies to be slaughtered within days to one month of birth for "bob" veal. Others are cruelly raised for months for "milk-fed" veal, and still others may be

No Milk of Human Kindness 167

transported long distances to be reared for cheap products like hamburger by the beef industry. But, because it's often not economically feasible to raise all these excess animals, calves who aren't used for veal or beef production may be sold for rendering to be turned into tallow, grease, or animal feed. Or, they're simply abandoned to starve to death, be shot, beaten to death, or buried alive by the producer.

Chapter 45

Years earlier, I had investigated conditions on dairy farms in California, photographing the mounds of dead calves and cows piled up by the roadside waiting for "dead trucks" to make their daily rounds. Now, we'd received a complaint about a mega-dairy farm in the Pacific Northwest. At my request, Bob Baker flew to Tacoma, Washington, where, with assistance from representatives of the United Farm Workers union, he was able to arrange a meeting with employees at that monstrous "farm."

On a sunny Saturday morning in April, Bob met with a group of twelve workers outside the local grange hall in town. Most of the men were in their twenties and thirties and of Mexican descent. Some spoke English, but, for those who didn't, Bob had recruited a local teenager named Ruben to serve as translator. Bob pulled a pad from his backpack and began taking notes. Ruben asked the workers to provide their names when they spoke.

Bull calves, said a worker who identified himself as Ramon, were considered nothing more than a waste product to the farm. Female calves, on the other hand, were more valuable to the operation because they were used as dairy replacement heifers.

"This is José," Ruben said. "He says the biggest problem at the dairy is that they let the baby Jerseys* starve to death. They leave the bull calves lying there. He says sometimes they'll go for like a week without ever feeding them. And a lot of them starve to death every day."

---

* Jersey cows are the smallest dairy breed whereas Holsteins are the largest. Jerseys also have lower carcass yield and quality and therefore are less profitable for beef than Holsteins. This operation housed both Jerseys and Holsteins.

The other workers nodded their heads, agreeing that the farm's primary method of destroying thousands of unwanted, surplus Jersey bull calves was simply to let them starve.

"'Don't waste your time on them!' is all you hear from the bosses' mouths," said a worker named Alfredo. "But you can't just let them lie there and suffer and starve. But that's exactly what they want you to do." Even female calves deemed weak, he said, were left to starve to death.

Management, the workers said, left the unwanted calves lying outside the pens, shivering, despite it being warm outdoors. "They're sick," said a fourth worker. "They need help. They're too weak, too young to drink from a pail of milk. Nobody feeds them, and they die. They starve them first then they shoot the ones that haven't starved to death."

When supervisors would finally shoot the calves—which, according to the workers was usually done on the night shift—they would use a .22 caliber firearm. Sometimes the process would take several shots. "They don't die right away," explained an employee. "Some of them lie on the floor and bleed out for hours. There's usually always one still alive in the dead pile." He said that sometimes the calves would still be alive when he'd remove them by front-end loader.

"If a calf stands up or runs away after they shoot it," said another, "the supervisors pretend like they're 'hunting a wild animal'—just start shooting at it, hitting it anywhere they can. They do it for fun. One supervisor out there is really bad. Sometimes he'll grab a calf and say, 'Do you like this one? Should we save this one?' If you say yes, he shoots it right in front of you."

In some instances, the workers said, surplus calves were killed with blunt force trauma, a practice they called "bashing heads." They said that bashing heads with two-by-fours and poles had been standard practice until the press reportedly got a hold of the issue. Then, for a short time, the employees were instructed to bury the calves alive. "They're not burying them alive now," a worker explained. "But they still bash heads on the night shift."

Intimidation was often used to prevent employees from caring for the animals; the farm took advantage of the immigrants' undocumented status.

"They're constantly reminding you that you're undocumented," said one worker.

"They throw it in your face all the time," said another. When employees complained about the way in which the calves were treated, the worker shared, supervisors threatened them by saying that the dairy doesn't check immigration papers like other employers in the area.

The conversation shifted to the treatment of mature cows. "One supervisor is real mean to them. Last week, he was hitting cows with rocks to move them around in the hospital." The hospital is merely a series of pens where animals with mastitis, hoof problems, and other treatable conditions are held.

Despite there being a "hospital," as with calves, the workers said, most sick cows just laid on the ground until they starved to death or were shot. "Some cows have stuff bubbling from their mouths," explained a worker. "Management doesn't even care about them until they drop to the ground. And then they only care because they have to get rid of them."

"If a cow is sick and can't stand," Ruben spoke again for José, "she can't eat and she starves to death. He says they have what they call the 'junk pen.' They leave them in the junk pen to die."

"Most of the sick cows starve before supervisors ever get around to shooting them," said Alfredo. "Even if the sick cow is about to give birth, they still just let the mother and the unborn baby die—starve to death."

Without enough beds in the crowded barns, cows would lie in the filthy water used to flush barn floors. Mastitis was the predictable result. Adding insult to injury were insanitary conditions during milking and "manure and piss covered beds."

"When you feel their teats," said a milker, "they're real hot. They're all swollen and infected. Pus comes out. They smell really bad and the milk is the texture of cottage cheese."

"The boss tells workers to milk the cows even if they know the milk is bad," added another. "The milk will look like pieces of cheese. The boss says that bad milk will be mixed with much more good milk, so it's okay."

No Milk of Human Kindness 171

Even though there are no known veterinary references regarding the removal of any of a cow's four teats for treating mastitis, the workers said that when cows suffered from persistent mastitis, supervisors would use a razor-like device to cut a portion of the nipple off to drain the blood and pus from the infected udder. This excruciating procedure was performed without anesthetic causing the cows to cry out.

As for the thousands of "dry" or non-lactating cows who were housed outdoors on dirt lots, their only protection from the elements was metal roofs held up by wooden posts. "There isn't enough room for all the cows to get under the pole roof on the dry lots," said Alfredo. "It's sad to see how they try to block themselves from the sun in the summer—trying to find shade. But they can't find any."

As for the winter, "Some cows freeze to death on dry lots," Alfredo continued. "They lie there stiff. Sometimes you think they're sleeping, but when you're cleaning and you go to nudge them out of your way, you realize that they're dead."

Chapter 46

Two of the workers Bob had interviewed agreed to carry cameras into the facility and document violations for HFA. As in the past, we welcomed any photographic evidence we could get. At the same time, Bob wanted to see firsthand some of what the workers had described.

Driving a rented pickup, Bob gained access to the vast dairy farm complex through a side entrance. He drove for a few miles, then saw the enormous, open dairy barns—each the length of a few football fields.

On closer inspection, the barn floors were filthy, covered with standing flush water, just as the workers had described, and cows were lying on the wet concrete floors. Behind the barns, Bob found the dry lots, with cows as far as the eye could see.

Next, he ventured into an area where one of the employees he had spoken with worked. There, eight newborn calves were confined in a pen. Four bull calves lay listlessly outside the pen. Bob photographed one of the calves, who was lying on his side. When he squatted down to shoot another photo, a second calf struggled to his feet. Emaciated and weak, he wobbled over to Bob.

Bob petted the newborn, who in turn licked his hand with his warm, rough tongue. Because mother cows lick and clean their young, it seemed that the simple gesture of petting the calf caused the baby to become attached to Bob. As Bob walked back to the pickup, parked several hundred feet away on the other side of the road, the little calf tagged along. Bob repeatedly turned to shoo the calf away, but he kept coming, following the investigator to the pickup. Bob called to the worker who retrieved the emaciated animal and carried him back to the pen area.

No Milk of Human Kindness 173

Later that evening, Bob telephoned me and told me every detail of the encounter. Abandoning the newborn, he said, its huge brown eyes pleading for food and affection, was one of the most challenging experiences of his career.

While Bob had desperately wanted to rescue that poor calf, he couldn't do so without blowing his cover. He needed to be able to access the facility again to document ongoing abuses. As in so many of our cases, we often had to make a Sophie's choice—leaving one or more suffering animals behind in the hopes of saving more victims down the road.

The following day, the worker told Bob that the calf—who hadn't been permitted to suckle on his mother even one time—was dead. Starvation. Just one of thousands of victims of starvation at the farm.

Chapter 47

As with the other cases, Bob and I worked feverishly to compile a complaint replete with worker testimony, graphic photographs, and a summary of state laws being violated. Again, aware that the county district attorney would likely decline to prosecute one of the region's biggest employers, we filed our petition with the Oregon attorney general.

So why, then, did we keep banging our heads against the same brick wall reaching out to attorneys general, the top legal officers in the states? Because, other than notifying law enforcement authorities and the media of violations—the two approaches we took—there was, quite frankly, nowhere else to turn. There was always the possibility that an attorney general would take our evidence seriously. You can only strike out so many times. Or *can* you?

It took the attorney general's Office nine long months to respond to our petition.

"We have conferred with the county District Attorney," wrote the AG in response to further pressure from HFA. "He informed us that two years ago his office evaluated allegations of alleged [head bashing] at the farm. No criminal charges were filed as a result of that investigation." As far as we were concerned, the fact that such allegations had previously surfaced only *strengthened* our case.

The letter went on to say that a sheriff's deputy had investigated an earlier complaint about abuse to cows lodged by a local animal rescue group. Based on "available evidence and witnesses," the officer had concluded that the complaint was "unfounded." HFA would learn that the deputy had apparently failed to interview any Spanish-speaking, non-management employees during his perfunctory investigation.

174

No Milk of Human Kindness 175

The final reason the AG refused to prosecute was because "HFA's original report was not retained by this department." The AG had indicated in his letter that HFA's sixty-four-page complaint and supporting documentation were either discarded or destroyed by his office. This was an extraordinary admission. The rationale for not prosecuting the offenders was that the AG had destroyed the evidence!

Days after receiving a copy of the Attorney General's letter, the mega-dairy farm issued a press release stating that "HFA's unfounded charges were insulting to our hardworking, valuable employees who care for our livestock using best practices to assure the health of the herd. Hopefully the Humane Farming Association's reckless disregard for the truth will not cause irreparable damage to consumer confidence in the safety of the State's agricultural products or the high standards state dairies practice in preserving animal welfare."

HFA followed up by running full-page ads in newspapers throughout the Pacific Northwest. The photo at the top of the page depicted a newborn bull calf at the farm who had died of starvation. The headline read:

NO MILK OF HUMAN KINDNESS FOUND HERE

"The Attorney General has been provided with worker statements as well as extensive photographic documentation," read the ad. "Inexplicably, after sitting on the evidence for nine months, it is now apparent that the Office of the Attorney General destroyed or discarded the extensive evidence of animal cruelty that was provided to it. Some believe that the Attorney General is fearful of investigating a well-funded and politically influential agribusiness corporation."

That summer, we heard from the workers that the dairy farm reduced its herd size by seven thousand animals, and instituted policies for the handling of unwanted male calves. Management agreed to stop starving the animals, selling them to calf buyers instead. Cameras were apparently installed in barns to monitor workers' treatment of cows (or, more likely, to ensure that workers weren't videotaping violations). In addition, following

HFA's investigation, the United Farm Workers negotiated a contract with the facility. It was the first major union agreement ever negotiated for dairy farm workers in the state. In addition to improving working conditions, the contract included a stipulation specifying that employees could not be disciplined or retaliated against for reporting animal abuse. This was a significant and precedent-setting accomplishment. Given law enforcement's predilection to protect the dairy farm, this was about the best we could have hoped for.

Chapter 48

I had been receiving neurofeedback for months in Asheville; neurofeedback is a kind of biofeedback in which sensors are applied to the scalp. The patient watches an interactive video on a computer screen and the sensors provide real-time data on brain activity. Over the course of a few dozen sessions, neurofeedback is supposed to train the brain to relax.

It wasn't working.

The doctor performing neurofeedback on me in Asheville suggested that I travel to California to get more help. The neuroscientist inventor of neurofeedback was located in the Los Angeles area. Accompanied by my faithful and devoted Asheville friend, Gideon, I headed west.

Despite my scheduled appointments, the neuroscientist couldn't see me as planned. For the most part, Gid and I set up camp at Bradley Miller's brother's apartment on the outskirts of Los Angeles. It was very generous of Brad's brother to open his home to me and my friend.

By now, I had dropped twenty pounds. I was experiencing glare, shimmering, floaters, tinnitus, migraines, and disorientation. There we were, stuck in Los Angeles, and I, once again didn't know where to turn.

In desperation, I returned to UCLA where doctors had at least given me a definitive diagnosis. After additional testing by yet more ophthalmologists and neurologists, my cone dystrophy proved stable, and no doctor there was able to provide further help.

Next, I embarked on a wild goose chase. My Asheville doctor recommended that, while waiting for the neuroscientist in Los Angeles, I visit yet another neurofeedback practitioner, this one in Washington State. So, while Gideon headed home to North Carolina, I took a northbound train to Seattle. Once there, while staying in the unoccupied home of a friend, I received four weeks of neurofeedback. It had no effect.

Bob Baker, at Bradley's request, eventually flew to Seattle to "collect" me, and then drove me back to Los Angeles to see the neuroscientist there. I was treated unsuccessfully with neurofeedback for yet another two months.

During his brief time with me in Los Angeles, Bob also accompanied me to the renowned Amen Clinic, about an hour and a half south of LA. It was one of ten Amen Clinics in the United States. Using brain SPECT imaging, which measures blood flow and activity in the brain both at rest and during a concentration task, the doctors there analyzed my brain function. They prescribed a medication that affects brain neurotransmitters; it would take time to see if that drug would help.

As an aside, it wasn't only Bradley Miller's brother who showed me kindness by housing me while I was based in Los Angeles. Brad, himself, continued to support me throughout this unending drama. When I called him from LA one afternoon because I was immobilized with fear, didn't know where to turn or what to do, he demonstrated incredible compassion and talked me down off a cliff.

One afternoon, amidst all the madness I was experiencing in Los Angeles, I received a cell phone call from the president of the Animal Welfare Institute in Washington, DC. That was the same Animal Welfare Institute where I had worked twenty years earlier for Christine Stevens. Sadly, Christine had passed away in 2002 at the age of eighty-four. She had left the organization in the capable hands of Cathy Liss, her protégé.

Cathy was calling to inform me that I had been selected to be the recipient of the Albert Schweitzer Medal for my "achievement in the advancement of animal welfare."

The medal had been given to Dr. Schweitzer himself, environmentalist Rachel Carson, Dr. Jane Goodall, Senator Robert Dole, US Supreme Court Justice Abe Fortas, and others, and now it was being awarded to me. The

No Milk of Human Kindness 179

ceremony, which was scheduled to take place in four months, would be held in a Congressional hearing room in the US Capitol complex.

I had attended an Albert Schweitzer Medal ceremony back when I was twenty-eight years old; at the time, I felt like I had arrived. *Now I was to be the honoree?*

Now, back in Asheville, I laid on an exam table in my local doctor's office where a nurse administered "liquid gold." A research scientist at an Oregon university had analyzed a sample of my blood and had found an unusual antibody in my eyes. She'd suggested treatment with intravenous immunoglobulin (IVIG), a powerful anti-inflammatory. One dose of IVIG—which comes from human plasma—is derived from thousands of donors.

It took five long hours for the product to drip into my veins. Remarkably, over the next month, the treatment seemed to reduce the inflammation I'd been experiencing. Whether it would ease any of my eye symptoms was something that remained to be seen.

Chapter 49

The Directors of the Animal Welfare Institute
request the honor of your presence
at the presentation of the
Albert Schweitzer Medal
To
Gail A. Eisnitz
By
John Mackey, Chief Executive Officer
Whole Foods Market

So read the invitation to one hundred or so dignitaries, media, friends, and family members to attend the presentation of the Albert Schweitzer Medal in the Russell Senate Office Building, the oldest congressional office building on Capitol Hill. According to a press release issued in advance of the presentation, "In the course of her work as an investigator, Gail has been chased, harassed, and threatened with bodily harm," said Animal Welfare Institute President Cathy Liss. "She has earned the respect of and negotiated strategic alliances with slaughterhouse workers and their union representatives during her tireless efforts to expose egregious crimes against animals."

". . . John Mackey, CEO of Whole Foods Markets, will present the medal. Whole Foods Markets is the world's largest natural and organic foods supermarket chain. . . ."

I was forty-eight years old now and I was thrilled.

Dressed in black velvet pants, short matching jacket, with a gauzy camisole underneath, I entered the historic hearing room with my family and my

No Milk of Human Kindness   181

friend Gideon at my side. In the chamber, a hundred plus attendees were
milling about. A photographer was busy flashing pictures. A cornucopia of
fresh fruits and vegetables—bananas, eggplants, lettuces, pears, pumpkins,
radishes, parsley—provided by Whole Foods Market and artfully arranged
on long wooden tables, graced the entire width of the formal caucus room.
Cathy Liss had seen to it that my giant star quilt, gifted to me by Rosebud
Sioux Tribal members for my efforts in stopping construction of the hog
factory, was hanging along one wall. The wood paneled walls, lofty ceilings,
blue patterned carpet, and dimly lit chandeliers of the ornate hearing room
made for an opulent setting.

And I was immediately overwhelmed.

Not emotionally, as I should have been. Rather, I was overwhelmed
visually by the patterns, the lighting, and the motion of the attendees milling
about. In much the way the tangle of tree branches in the forest conspired to
hijack my senses when hiking, the hearing room was too much for my brain
to process. Everything was chaos to me.

Panicked and almost unable to speak coherently, I headed directly over
to the complimentary wine bar where a bartender poured me a large plastic
goblet of Chardonnay. I had hoped that a glass of wine would calm me, relax
my vision, and help me get through the ceremony. I gulped down the wine,
but it didn't seem to do the job.

As the ceremony got underway, I was called to the podium. First, there
was a warm introduction by Cathy Liss. Next, I was surprised to see federal meat inspectors' union representative, and now friend, Gary Dahl, step
forward. He lauded my association with his union's members, and then
presented me with an appreciation plaque.

Finally, Whole Foods Markets CEO John Mackey made his way to
the microphone. He spoke eloquently about Dr. Schweitzer's legacy and
philosophy of "reverence for life" that extended to all creatures. And then
he turned to me.

"Ladies and gentlemen," he said, "Gail Ann Eisnitz is a hero—or if you
prefer the feminine rendition—she is a heroine. She has passion, she has
courage, she has integrity, and she has consistently acted in ways to help

182 OUT OF SIGHT

animals. Few people I have ever met can possibly compare with her. She is a great heroine on behalf of animals."

Mackey went on to give a thirty-minute speech highlighting my career achievements, praising and celebrating my victories. I was deeply humbled, but I was petrified, feeling exactly as I had thirty-three long years earlier on my high school gymnasium basketball court.

Good thing I had a prepared speech . . . or so I thought. I usually talk fervently off the cuff with notes in hand. But in this case—the apex of my achievements, the culmination of my career—my speech was not delivered by a "great heroine on behalf of animals" but by a woman who couldn't process her whereabouts.

My oratory skills went south; my impassioned plea on behalf of suffering animals went out the window. Instead, for thirty-five interminable minutes, I found myself droning on, reciting my speech, flat and emotionless, as if I were reading from the telephone book.

The content of the speech was powerful but the delivery must have seemed uninspired. I'd given dozens of rousing presentations in my career, yet, this time, I was humiliated and mortified beyond words.

And, still, I received a standing ovation.

Those in attendance that night must have known I was a bit off the mark, I was not at the top of my game. But nobody in the crowd celebrating my accomplishments that evening was aware, until now, that I was barely functioning—my perception and my very being befuddled—and even I did not know why.

Part Seven

A Prosecutor Steps to the Plate

Chapter 50

Months later, Ingrid DiMarino, an employee at an Ohio pig farm, contacted HFA with a shocking complaint. She said that coworkers at the farm where she worked were killing sick and injured breeding sows by hanging them. Yes, hanging.

The undercover video that HFA would ultimately obtain would depict downed sows at the operation, prior to hanging, being kicked, shocked, poked, and dragged down the barn's alleyway. Some emitted ear-piercing screams and feebly shook their heads until, eventually defeated, they stopped vocalizing and resisting altogether, unable to struggle anymore.

Once at the barn door, the animals were then pushed off a four-foot ledge onto a pile of disabled and dead sows on the cold earth. One particular sow remained splayed out atop the pile—her spine protruding and face scarred. She waited for more than half an hour in the frigid winter air, shivering, before the workers finally got to her. She watched, ears droopy, apparently resigned to her fate, as her fellow victims were hanged.

When it was her turn, the workers fastened a chain around her neck; the other end of the chain was hooked to the fork on a front-end loader.

An employee operating the tractor lifted the fork. When the tines were raised, the sow struggled violently, until she eventually suffocated under the weight of her own body.

This was Ingrid's reason for contacting HFA but, we would learn, it was by no means the only atrocity taking place at this operation.

"What do workers do when the sows collapse in the crates or the pens?" I asked Ingrid during an initial interview.

"They leave them to starve to death, or shoot them, or they hang them," she replied. She further explained that pigs who were sick, weak, injured, or emaciated were rarely, if ever, provided veterinary care. Instead, sows were abandoned to die, be cannibalized, or, if salvageable, shipped out for sale.

"If they're hurt or sick and can't walk," Ingrid said, "they just leave them. No food, no water. Sometimes the guys will throw food to them, but they can't get it. It usually just ends up on their head or in their eyes."

I'd heard it all before.

"And they can't get to the waterers—they're too high. If they do drag themselves there, they can't reach it. So, they basically lay there until they just waste away to skeletons."

Ingrid had complained vociferously to the farm's owner about the hangings, suggesting that even a gunshot to the hog's head would be less barbaric. "So, then they decided they would just use them for target practice. And they just shoot them wherever. And sometimes they're not even dead when they're done. And then they drag them and throw them in the dead hole alive.

"This one kid said to me, 'Joe, the farm manager, shot one that had laid there for eight days—he shot her thirteen times.' And then he apparently hooked her to the back of the truck with a chain and dragged her down the gravel road."

With Ingrid's support, "Pete," a seasoned undercover investigator working with HFA, posed as her cousin and quickly landed a job at the farm. Over the course of two months, both Pete and Ingrid, armed with cameras, obtained video evidence and kept detailed notes. They documented hundreds upon hundreds of violations.

When all was said and done, Pete and Ingrid had succeeded in shooting photos and video of filthy, overcrowded pens; insect-infested feed bins; dead piglets floating in waste pits; newborns being callously tossed into carts and transport vehicles; pigs with fractured bones, huge open sores, and emaciation; and dead sows who had been abandoned inside crates or whose remains appeared to have melted into pen floors.

A Prosecutor Steps to the Plate

But it was the video that Pete shot, of sows being hanged, that provided the most definitive evidence of violations of Ohio's anti-cruelty statutes.

"During the first hanging," wrote Pete in his field notes, "it took five minutes for the sow to stop kicking. The sow thrashed in circles and kicked violently and then, after several minutes, she wobbled from side to side, and slightly jerked before becoming still."

Forced to bear more than two litters per year, she had spent her life inside a twenty-inch-wide crate. Now this.

In the video, unaware he was being recorded, the worker operating the front-end loader left the controls, ran up and placed his arms around the sow's large girth, and began hugging the dead animal, a huge smile on his face, all the while she was dangling from the tine. Two other workers looked on, laughing at his antics, clearly pleased at their accomplishment.

The hanging procedure was repeated two more times that afternoon, as helpless sows had the chain fastened around their necks and were strung up alive.

Chapter 51

In preparation for the strong case we knew we had, I quickly typed up Pete and Ingrid's notes and transcribed all recorded interviews. Again, Bob and I worked around the clock preparing a complaint replete with a summary of violations at the hog farm and incorporating photographs of scores of dying and dead sows, including those who had been hanged. We did our homework and learned that the Ohio attorney general's office did not have prosecutorial jurisdiction in criminal cases like ours. This time, our target would have to be the county prosecutor.

The writing was on the wall after local authorities conducted a raid and searched the premises. They initially gave the hog producer a mere "warning"—a slap on the wrist—for the violations at his farm. Although HFA stood ready to take hundreds of animals to its rescue farm, not a single animal was seized.

Then, perhaps because these abuses took place in "farm country," perhaps because the hog farmer's daughter worked as an attorney in the prosecutor's office, the county prosecutor did everything in his power to bury the case.

Because of the conflict with the farmer's daughter, HFA was able to press for a change of venue in the case. We succeeded, and the case was transferred to a special prosecutor in the nearby city of Canton.

INJURED AND HELPLESS.
HER PROBLEMS HAVE ONLY JUST BEGUN . . .

So read the headline which appeared under a photo of a downed sow, her eyes staring helplessly into the camera lens. It was a full-page ad that HFA ran in twenty-eight Ohio newspapers.

"This sow is in grave danger," the ad continued. "Some of her pen mates have been dragged from their sick pens and had a chain placed around their necks. A front-end loader was used to lift the chain, slowly strangling them to death." A photo of two dead sows hanging from the tines of a front-end loader accompanied the text.

The advertisement urged readers to contact the special prosecutor, Frank Forchione, asking him to prosecute those responsible for the crimes to the fullest extent of the law.

"Frank Forchione has handled numerous cases involving treatment of animals in twenty years as a prosecuting attorney," read a follow-up news story that appeared in a local newspaper.[1] "But the longtime Canton prosecutor was overwhelmed by the avalanche of responses he received" from the ad.

"I got hundreds of emails, phone calls at my office, and even phone calls at my home," Forchione said in the story. "I knew when I agreed to handle this case as a special prosecutor that it involved animals, but I never imagined the magnitude and effect it would have on people."

And so Special Prosecutor Forchione was spurred into action.

The local magistrate refused to sign off on a search warrant to get additional evidence; Forchione was not permitted access to the hog farm. Still, according to another newspaper story, Forchione said, "'After reviewing the footage shot by the employees and hearing from witnesses in interview, it didn't matter whether I was able to set foot on the farm. Obviously, what was going on was disturbing.'"[2]

Forchione then uttered the words we had been waiting for years to hear from a prosecutor: "I just decided at that point that *somebody has to speak up for the voiceless* [emphasis added]."[3] And again, in yet another paper: "*Someone needs to speak up for the voiceless* [emphasis added]. It's just as serious as some of the other crimes we deal with on a daily basis."[4]

And speak up he did. After about a month's preparation, Forchione filed charges in the case. Ten counts of animal cruelty, to be exact. The farm owner was charged with two counts for failing to provide appropriate care to ill animals and failing to provide adequate shelter, food, and water to pigs. His son—the farm manager—was slapped with six counts for grabbing weanlings by their ears and hurling them through the air into transport vehicles, thumping piglets, hanging sows, and other offenses. And the farmhand who had been mugging for his friends as he hugged a hanged sow was arraigned on two counts of beating and torturing animals.

Not surprisingly, both Ingrid and Pete were subjected to intense witness intimidation, Ingrid by farm employees and Pete by local law enforcement authorities. Likewise, the entire farming community was in the hog producer's camp. According to the local newspaper, more than four hundred people attended a fundraiser for him. The paper explained that an earlier fundraiser had drawn another four hundred supporters and netted thousands of dollars toward the hog farmer's legal bills.[5]

By now, HFA was in contact with producers of documentaries for HBO. They were interested in exposing the case on national TV.

Chapter 52

And so, deciding to attend this precedent-setting trial, Bradley Miller, Bob Baker, and I wound up at the county courthouse—located smack dab in the heart of Ohio farm country. Bob had kindly picked me up at the airport, and driven me to the court.

The big brick courthouse was a modern building with a semicircular staircase that led up to the courtroom. HBO's videographer—his camera and tripod—was stationed in the front of the courtroom, where he had a straight shot of the defendants, the witness stand, and the judge's bench.

All three defendants were seated at the witness table, each with his own attorney. What was conspicuously missing was the jury. The defendants had waived their right to a jury trial. They weren't stupid. The judge—a farmer who had previously refused to issue arrest warrants in the case and had told Forchione that he never should have filed charges—would likely be sympathetic to their cause, so they strategically chose him over a jury of their peers.

The trial got underway.

On the witness stand, Pete explained for the prosecution how he had obtained the evidence and described conditions on the farm. He was subjected to intense grilling during cross examination by the defense.

Several other prosecution witnesses took the stand and explained what they encountered during the raid. A veterinarian and swine specialist from The Ohio State University stated that, during the search, he observed over forty sows that were in need of immediate veterinary care.

"Sows that were crippled, fractured spines, broken legs, things like that," he explained. "If they couldn't be rehabilitated in a timely fashion, a decision should be made for euthanasia. And it was apparent that many of them had been there for quite some time."

"When you spoke with the farm owner," asked Forchione, "did he describe what type of euthanasia was being done on that farm?"

"He acknowledged that they euthanized sows by hanging them. They also euthanized sows by gunshot. And they also used a sharp blow on baby pigs to euthanize them."

"Did you give him any advice when you were told that they were hanging pigs?"

"I told him hanging sows wasn't appropriate."

After a grueling first day of testimony, Forchione and his fellow prosecutors met with Pete, Brad, Bob, and me to discuss the trial's progress.

"It all boils down to whether this judge thinks hanging these pigs is bad," Forchione explained. "That's it. He's a farmer. He's told us he's a farmer. This is a rural community down here. We're not friendly faces."

Pete was off in his own world, and quietly responded, "It all boils down to the fact that, in our culture, one animal is lucky enough to be born a companion animal like a dog or cat. Another is unlucky enough to be born food."

Chapter 53

The following day it was the defense's turn to present its case. Unable to prevent our powerful video from being admitted into evidence, the defense resorted to the claim that the sows who were hanged and struggling for five minutes were not suffering. To do this, the defense had to go all the way to Iowa to find their "expert" witness in the person of one Dr. Paul Armbrecht, a veterinarian.

"My opinion," Armbrecht said in his paid testimony, "is that the method of using asphyxia via strangulation as was seen, that's *not* torture of the animal when the animal loses consciousness or it should and did appear to lose consciousness in a very short time period. That's not torture."

"So, then would it be fair to say," defense counsel asked, "that you did not observe any animal cruelty or torture as those terms are defined by the Court?"

"No sir, I did not."

Forchione stepped forward to cross-examine the witness. Under questioning, it became apparent that Armbrecht had no firsthand experience at the farm. He had neither talked to the defendants about their practices nor to anyone who had attended the search. The fact was, he had never even been to the operation.

Forchione asked the judge if he could show a video clip. The judge nodded.

The lights were turned down. There was dead silence in the courtroom. On a big screen, the images of a sow dangling alive from the fork of the front-end loader kept the audience spellbound.

194 OUT OF SIGHT

"By the way," said Forchione, "as we're watching, does that pig appear to be suffering?"

"I don't know whether it's suffering or not," Armbrecht responded.

"You're watching this video, sir. You saw that pig being hung and that pig struggling. *Is that pig suffering?*" Forchione pressed.

"I can't determine if that was suffering because we just can't tell very easily on that definition."

The video stopped. The lights came back on.

"Just from what you observed, is that a proper manner of euthanasia? *Is that a proper manner of euthanasia?*" Forchione repeated louder.

"Yes, sir," Armbrecht replied.

"Was that animal suffering?"

"I don't think it was."

"You don't think that what we just watched was that animal suffering?"

"No, sir."

With the judge's permission, Forchione then handed some papers to Armbrecht. It was a copy of the farm owner's initial statement to the sheriff's department. "Top of page five," Forchione instructed the witness, "The operator was asked, 'What about a plan concerning euthanasia?' What was his response?"

"'We hang our sows like they do people in Utah,'" Armbrecht read from the statement.

"Does it mention anywhere in his statement that they were doing it to try to minimize the pain of the animal?"

"No, sir," said Armbrecht.

"It's not mentioned at all. It talks about that it's going to hang this sow like they do people in Utah."

"I have some questions for this witness," the judge interjected, leaning forward on clasped hands. He proceeded to ask for clarification about the pig who appeared in the video. It had been dragged a distance, he said, had

A Prosecutor Steps to the Plate

been pushed off a four-foot ledge and then was picked up by its neck with a chain. "Is that cruelty?"

"I don't think it's cruelty," replied Armbrecht.

"There was testimony by one of the defendants that it took four to five minutes for that animal to die. Is that cruelty to an animal?" the judge asked again.

"Even gassing hogs to death, it takes three to ten minutes," answered Armbrecht.

"An animal was allowed to lie there, and after the two days, in fact, dies naturally. Is that cruelty?" The judge was referring to the farm's so-called policy of allowing pigs to languish for *two days*. Two weeks was more like it.

"No."

"Thank you."

Chapter 54

The owner of the hog farm was the next, and only other, witness to testify for the defense. He took the stand, a vein bulging in his forehead as he chewed a wad of gum.

"If not for the Humane Farming Association and its undercover video," said Prosecutor Forchione, "we would not have become aware of what was going on at your farm, would we?"

"There is *no abuse* at my farm," he said angrily.

"Had Pete not worked for you, we would not have been able to see this footage and become aware of what was going on at your farm, now would we?"

"There is *no abuse* at my farm," the hog producer repeated.

Forchione moved on. "In your seven-page statement to the sheriff, is there any mention of any protocol regarding euthanasia?"

"Uh, I think I did mention that we hang sows."

"You said, '*We hang our sows like they do people in Utah.*' What do you mean by that?"

"It was a mistake." The farmer mumbled something inaudible.

"What do you mean by that? You stated, 'No, we hang our sows like they do people in Utah.' You just said that was a mistake. What do you mean by that?"

"It was State of Washington."

"Oh, so instead of Utah—"

"Instead of Utah, it was Washington."

Forchione shifted his line of questioning. The video Pete had shot also showed workers grabbing weanling pigs from their mothers' sides in farrowing crates and throwing them six feet into carts and, later, into transport vehicles.

A Prosecutor Steps to the Plate 197

"Is there any training how these piglets are tossed into carts or anything like that?" Forchione asked.

The farmer replied that his employees learned by watching him.

"You taught them to grab them by the ears and toss them like that? Do you have any concerns for the animals?"

"Yes. They're my only income."

"But *do you have any concerns for them?*" Forchione reiterated. "The pain that they're suffering or anything like that?"

"My pigs aren't suffering pain, *sir*," the farmer said, now openly glaring at the prosecutor.

"They're not suffering pain?"

He responded no.

"When we watched that pig being hanged, and we watched those legs kicking, and we saw those arms going like that, twisting. You don't think that pig was suffering in any way, shape, or form?"

"We euthanize our animals in the most efficient and painless way that we can."

"I'm going to ask you that question again. Was that animal suffering as its hands were going and its legs were going? *Was that animal suffering, sir?*"

"Have you ever seen a pig shot?"

"That's not my question to you. Was that animal suffering?"

"Not to my knowledge."

"I have no further questions, Your Honor."

Chapter 55

With the exception of the verdict, the court proceedings were now complete. The judge stated that he would take the testimony under consideration and review the video clips and other evidence that had been presented to the Court. He then promised to render his decision later in the day. Bob, Brad, and I cooled our heels for a few hours until a messenger informed us that the verdict was in and we walked quickly back to the courthouse.

The judge entered the courtroom from a front passageway. Again, there was dead silence. He seated himself behind the imposing wooden desk and began his remarks. I held my breath.

With regard to the farm owner, "as to the offense of cruelty to animals by not providing appropriate food and water, the Court finds that the defendant is *not guilty* of that offense as charged." Brad and I looked at each other and shook our heads in disgust.

With regard to the farmer's son, "as to the offense of cruelty to animals by improperly carrying or transporting said animals, the Court finds the defendant is *guilty* of that offense as charged."

Our hopes shot back up. The judge had just found the farm manager guilty of tossing piglets into carts in an inhumane fashion. Surely, he would convict the defendants for the hanging deaths of sows.

"As to the count in the same complaint, cruelty to animals by torture"— by torture, the judge meant "hanging"—"the Court finds the defendant is *not guilty* of that offense as charged."

Brad and I looked at each other again. My mouth was hanging open.

Now there was just the matter of whether the employee who had mugged for the hidden camera as he was hugging a strangled sow would be found guilty for hanging sows. All the other counts had been dismissed.

Regarding the count against the worker, "that being the remaining count of cruelty to animals by torture, the Court finds the defendant is *not guilty* of that offense as charged."

Brad, Bob, and I looked at each other in disbelief.

All through the trial I'd felt like we were on the precipice of something bigger than ourselves, something historic. In my naiveté, I felt certain that the lynching of breeding sows—animals in the service of man—was going to wake up the courts, and society, to a new dawn for animals. Finally, I thought, we were going to set a legal precedent mandating that animals have some very basic, intrinsic rights. Simply put, that animals have the right to not be strung up by their necks and slowly strangled.

I was wrong.

"Clearly, in my opinion," the judge expounded upon his decision, "there's no easy, safe, economical way to euthanize an adult hog. Disposing of the hog that was in the video was an attempt to alleviate pain in an animal that could not be saved," said the farmer/judge. "I find it personally distasteful that that, in fact, was done. But it is totally unrealistic to have a vet come out all the time and administer chemicals which seems to be the best way, but also the most expensive way, to dispose of an animal.

"The sentence of the Court," he continued, "will be a fine of $250 in costs. The defendant is placed under basic probation for the period of one year. They shall undergo a training program on the humane handling and transporting of farm animals. Obviously, there needs to be some review and reformulation of policies in order to avoid this in the future."

"Anything further from either counsel?"

"No, your honor."

"That will be all."

Chapter 56

Thankfully, this story didn't end in the courtroom. The fallout from the trial far exceeded our expectations. As the court proceedings were covered by local television affiliates, footage from the farm aired repeatedly on Cleveland TV, reaching thousands of viewers. It was gratifying to know that, even though he escaped fines in court, the hog producer complained that he'd spent an estimated $77,000 in legal expenses[1]—much more than criminal fines he could have incurred.

HBO produced an astounding hour and a half long documentary about the investigation and ensuing trial entitled *Death on a Factory Farm*. The feature showed never-before-seen-on-television footage of sows confined in gestation and farrowing crates; weanlings being hurled into bins and transport vehicles; piglets being thumped; buckets overflowing with dead newborns; and animals engaging in cannibalism. The HBO documentary then included repeated images of the hangings, key witness testimony shot during the trial, and the judge's verdict.

HBO broadcast *Death on a Factory Farm* more than nineteen times over the course of a month and then many more times that year. The program reached millions of viewers who otherwise would have never known what goes on behind the closed doors of America's factory farms.

And the investigation put thousands of farmers on notice. "The public is scrutinizing everything about farming," read an editorial in a well-known farm trade publication. "The Humane Farming Association came from California to Ohio to pick this fight. Who knew they were even watching? Your farm could be the next one blindsided and in the crosshairs of the pro-animal movement. Is someone watching you? Could you handle the

A Prosecutor Steps to the Plate 201

scrutiny? Are you prepared to explain yourself and all the things that you do?"[2]

"We've been at this for over twenty-five years," Bradley Miller said on camera at the conclusion of the HBO documentary, "so we look at it pretty realistically. And that's why, even though there was only one conviction in this case, it has to be viewed as progress. It has to be a vindication and a validation of undercover anti-cruelty investigations. There have been people all across this country who have seen this videotape footage. It has been a window into the daily operations of the pork industry in this country."

There is one important footnote. Special Prosecutor Frank Forchione, the only attorney we'd ever encountered who felt compelled to enforce the law and "speak up for the voiceless," was shortly thereafter elected to the post of esteemed judge in the Stark County, Ohio, Court of Common Pleas. Today he is referred to as The Honorable Frank G. Forchione.

Part Eight

Connecting the Dots

Chapter 57

"Mommy, why is the world made up of dots?" I had asked my mother when I was five years old. When I grew older, I stopped questioning my pixelated view of the world. It was my normal.

As the years had passed, my visual processing problem and headaches had diminished somewhat. Between the drug prescribed by the Amen Clinic and the IVIG—both powerful anti-inflammatories—the confusion had lessened to a certain degree. While disorientation would rear its ugly head every now and again, it wasn't nearly as disabling as it had been.

The dots, glare, floaters, night blindness, and tinnitus, on the other hand, had all gotten worse. Sometimes I felt like I was in a fish tank—all the splotches floating around me were so disruptive. I could no longer drive at night; car headlights had giant halos around them, making it impossible to negotiate the road. While tinnitus generally occurs independent of other issues, this was different. The ringing in my ears reminded me of the shimmering in my eyes. I knew there was a correlation. I could feel it.

I had long ago stopped going to doctors to find a cure, but I still wanted to know what was wrong with me.

In my countless Google searches over the years to find resolution to my visual problem, I had encountered a small minority of people who suffered from what they called "snowy vision." I understood that snowy vision was a condition in which one's entire visual field is suffused with what looks like television static. Dots. *Dots.* I had found no scientific papers, no diagnoses on the subject, only a handful of personal stories recounted by those afflicted by it. I didn't know who these people were or why they suffered, but I knew they were my tribe.

It had been many years since I had researched my eye problem on the computer—I had all but given up. So, one steamy Saturday morning in August 2020, while sitting at my laptop at my dining room table, I randomly typed "snowy vision" into the Google search engine and pressed return. What popped up would rock my world.

"Visual Snow Syndrome." It was in the National Organization for Rare Disorders Rare Disease Database.

"Visual snow is a neurological disorder characterized by a continuous visual disturbance that occupies the entire visual field and is described as tiny flickering dots that resemble the noise of a detuned analogue television. In addition to the static, or 'snow,' affected individuals can experience additional visual symptoms such as sensitivity to light (photophobia); visual effects originating from within the eye itself (entoptic phenomena) and impaired night vision (nyctalopia)."[1]

My symptoms, exactly.

The explanation continued, "The prevalence of visual snow in the general population is currently unknown. The average age of the visual snow population seems to be younger than for many other neurological disorders. This early onset, combined with a general lack of recognition by health care providers, suggest it is an uncommon problem.

"Initial functional brain imaging research"—PET scans—"suggests visual snow is a brain disorder. Visual snow is a chronic, sometimes highly disabling, uncommon condition."

Next, I found and read the few published papers on the disorder, viewed a website dedicated to the syndrome, and visited a Facebook page. In my research, I learned that, in addition to experiencing the visual symptoms of extreme glare, floaters, and entoptic phenomena (in which one sees thousands of microscopic white blood cells that resemble tadpoles zipping across one's visual field), the majority of individuals with VSS also experienced ringing in the ears. Many had migraines, and some suffered from depersonalization—a persistent and terrifying feeling of altered reality in which one's surroundings appear unreal, unfamiliar, or strange.

Connecting the Dots

I also discovered that, while Visual Snow Syndrome is often seen in combination with migraine, researchers believe that it is a totally separate condition. VSS appears to be a complex neurological disorder linked to a hyperexcitability in the brain's visual cortex. Individuals with Visual Snow Syndrome experience a "disruption in the filtering and integration of incoming visual information," read one paper.[2] "The nerve cells in the brains of people with visual snow syndrome may be too responsive to visual stimuli," explained another. "These nerve cells mistakenly send signals to the brain. The brain interprets them as real images."[3]

I was stunned.

It took time for me to process what I had stumbled upon. After all, I had been grappling with the disorder for as long as I could remember. It had been a lifelong struggle.

Although embarrassing to admit—and I promised myself I would not reveal this figure—over the years I had seen more than one hundred physicians trying to resolve this problem. Some, whom you've met in this book, took me seriously. Many did not. None solved the mystery. I solved it by myself.

But now things were adding up. Looking back, I could see that a handful of doctors had actually been on the right trajectory. While my complaints to them generally concentrated on my eyes, some doctors knew to focus on my brain. The neuro-ophthalmologist at Johns Hopkins Medical Center had suggested that I schedule a PET scan; NYU neurologist Dr. Oliver Sacks indicated that I might have an area of cortical hypersensitivity; and the doctors at California's Amen Clinic had identified a problem area in my brain. They were essentially right.

But, why, then, hadn't they diagnosed me with Visual Snow Syndrome?

The fact is, not one of them had ever heard of it. They couldn't have. It didn't exist.

As it turns out, Visual Snow Syndrome wasn't identified or classified as a disease until 2014. VSS is so new and so rare that, even today, most ophthalmologists and neurologists have never heard of the disease.

I shared the information with my sister who was very excited. She said she recalled that, as a child, I spoke curiously of a world made up of dots. It was validating that she remembered. Over the next week, I slowly digested the enormity of the new information. And then I took action.

First, I wanted to confirm whether, in addition to suffering from the classic signs of Visual Snow Syndrome— static, glare, floaters, entoptic phenomena, and night blindness—individuals also experienced the perceptual disorientation that had plagued me for so long. So, I posed a simple question to members on the VSS Facebook page, asking whether those with the disorder had ever suffered from depersonalization or an altered state. I received a barrage of responses.

"VSS can make you feel almost like you're floating sometimes, and your surroundings can take on a dreamlike quality," read the first post.

"I constantly feel like I'm playing a video game instead of living. I know that the things around me are real and I can touch them, but it just doesn't feel like it," said the second.

"I often feel like I'm walking in a dream," wrote another.

"I see [my surroundings] like I have drunk six beers all the time," said yet a fourth. "I can't focus on my visual field. It's hell."

"I once tried to explain what it felt like to someone and they asked if I was on acid."

Exactly, I thought. And those were just a few of scores of similar comments.

While it was true that people with VSS experienced a lot of anxiety, my early research also revealed that they dealt with chronic inflammation, eye irritation, exhaustion, and other issues that had dogged me for so many years. What's more, some individuals on Facebook explained that visiting supermarkets and department stores was excruciating because of their sensitivity to fluorescent lighting. Others described a condition called "Alice in Wonderland Syndrome," an alteration of visual perception in which the sizes of external objects are perceived incorrectly. Although I had never shared that frightening symptom with anyone, I had routinely experienced it.

Connecting the Dots 209

Next, looking at the scientific papers, I concluded that the world's leading expert on Visual Snow Syndrome—essentially one of VSS pioneers who identified the syndrome in 2014—Dr. Peter Goadsby, was a professor and neurologist at King's College London. Because of the distance, he was out of the running as someone with whom I could consult.

On the VSS webpage, I homed in on a neuro-ophthalmologist at the University of Colorado School of Medicine, Denver, who was engaged in research on snowy vision. I composed what I thought was a compelling email to her. My hopes that I would hear back from her office were through the roof. Having seen so many physicians with so little satisfaction, understanding, or empathy, I was looking forward to speaking with one who could provide a definitive diagnosis, and, in so doing, validate my experience.

Weeks passed and I received no response to my email. When I phoned the university's School of Medicine and spoke with a scheduler, I was informed that I would have to provide a neurologist's referral and then survive a strict vetting process to determine if I was even a candidate to see this specialist. What doctor was going to refer me? As I said, most neurologists had never heard of Visual Snow Syndrome, not to mention that I was self-diagnosed. To say that I was deflated would be an understatement. My hopes were dashed. Once again, I felt like was back where I had started.

I let weeks pass as I wallowed in disappointment.

Then I got back on the stick. Something told me to research Dr. Goadsby again. Google and I conducted a deep dive, and, together we found that I had been mistaken—Dr. Goadsby was no longer in London after all. Instead, he was now a professor of neurology at the University of California, San Francisco.

I emailed him later that day. I explained that, in childhood, I had experienced staticky vision and, as an adult, I had suffered from all of the classic symptoms associated with the disease.

In addition, I explained, "I used to suffer from confusion and brain fog. For decades, I felt like I had severe dyslexia of the world. I suffered from spatial disorientation and a visual flooding problem that was affected by lighting levels, humidity, motion, etc., and caused a sense of confusion and a dreamlike state. After going through chemo and early menopause at age thirty-five, I also began having extreme eye fatigue and experiencing several headaches/migraines weekly."

I went on. "Over the years, I've had MRIs, EEGs, VERs, ERPs, and ERGs, I wore blurry glasses to reduce visual input, engaged in visual training and neurofeedback for two years each, and put myself in a psychiatric ward.

"As an aside," I continued, "I have managed to be a productive member of society and a published author in my field. Also, before I started my career, I worked as a textbook and magazine illustrator where I drew animals using tiny dots in much the way painter Georges Seurat used pointillism. I'm beginning to understand that this technique arose from the way I have always perceived the world in dots."

I concluded by saying that my disorientation and headaches had gotten somewhat better, but I explained that my classic VSS symptoms—like floaters, glare, and tinnitus—all seemed to be progressing.

And, since we were in the throes of the COVID-19 pandemic, I respectfully requested that we schedule a telehealth visit.

Dr. Goadsby emailed me back that very day.

As it turned out, he was now departing the University of California, San Francisco, bound for a new position at the renowned Goldberg Migraine Program at none other than UCLA.

In his email, Dr. Goadsby explained that it would be a few weeks before he would be settled in and taking on new patients. His team would reach out and contact me to schedule an appointment. He'd cc'd one Richard May on his email.

I was thrilled beyond words!

A month later, we had another email exchange during which Dr. Goadsby indicated he would be slightly delayed.

And then, radio silence . . . for four long months. I emailed again and sent a phone message through his scheduler. No response.

And then, one Thursday morning in February, when I was feeling particularly vulnerable and dejected, believing that my visual processing problem would never be diagnosed, I confided in my walking partner that I feared I

Connecting the Dots 211

had been blown off by yet another medical professional. It was almost more than I could bear.

Shortly after I returned home from my walk, my cell phone rang; the caller ID read "UCLA." I answered the call, and the man on the other end introduced himself as Richard. He had a very pleasant voice.

"I'm calling to tell you that Dr. Goadsby is settled in now," Richard said. "And he's scheduling his appointments," he continued. "He was wondering if you could see him on Tuesday. His colleague Dr. Pak will be on the appointment as well."

I had waited sixty years for this call.

My research indicated that Dr. Goadsby had just been chosen one of the recipients of the Brain Prize 2021—the world's largest and most celebrated award for outstanding achievement in neuroscience research.[4] He and three of his colleagues had been honored with the prestigious prize, and hundreds of thousands of dollars each, for their work unraveling the cause of migraines. As I saw it, he was also the "father of Visual Snow Syndrome."

I was a bundle of nerves when Tuesday rolled around. After all, how does one cram a lifetime of symptoms into one brief telehealth call. I had no idea how long the consult would be. Plus, I was used to perfunctory visits lasting mere minutes with doctors who invariably dismissed me, informing me that there was nothing they could do for me, or worse yet, that there was nothing wrong with me at all.

The moment I started talking with Dr. Goadsby and his colleague, I was put at ease, their empathy and compassion radiating through. The two neurologists spent close to an hour interviewing me. They wanted to know everything about me—from my weight to my migraine history to the color of the dots I see (they're black and white). After answering their long list of probing questions, I shared some of my own experiences.

"I went so far as to put myself in a rehab and in a psych ward in an attempt to solve my problem," I admitted. "You've got to understand, I was desperate."

OUT OF SIGHT

"I am *so sorry* that you had to do that," Dr. Goadsby replied in his lilting Australian accent. His genuine concern was a welcome departure from most of the physicians I had seen.

Dr. Goadsby and Dr. Pak asked me a few more follow up questions, and then the interview started to wind down. And then, near the end of our conversation, Dr. Goadsby suddenly uttered the words I had waited so long to hear.

"Well, I'll tell you, Gail," Dr. Goadsby said, "It's clear—it's *crystal clear*—that you have Visual Snow Syndrome."

"Crystal clear. *Crystal clear.*" Those words rang like a bell reverberating in my ears. They meant only one thing: *I was not crazy.*

Chapter 58

One cold January night, while watching the evening news, my interest was piqued when I saw a report on a major winter storm that had just ripped through northwestern Texas and eastern New Mexico. The correspondent said that "Winter Storm Goliath," as the blizzard was named, had dumped between eight and twenty-two inches of snow, with drifts in excess of fourteen feet. According to the reporter, it had claimed the lives of upwards of forty thousand dairy cows and calves in its path.

As soon as I woke the next morning, I started digging deeper. The majority of the animals in the hardest hit areas, it turned out, had been housed outside on dry lots without shelter. Windbreaks had been erected in some cases, but that wasn't enough to save their lives. Photos showed dead cattle partially buried under the snow. So, what was their cause of death? Most had suffocated in the snow.

The storm had been predicted a week in advance. The needless suffering and deaths had been entirely preventable had the animals just been provided basic shelter from the snow.

I started thinking about the dairy producers themselves. I wondered how they were able to sustain such exorbitant losses. I made some calls to government agriculture officials. That's when I first learned about USDA's Livestock Indemnity Program or "LIP."

LIP is a federal subsidy that pays livestock producers for animals who die in extreme weather — including winter storms, hurricanes, floods, hail, extreme heat, and extreme cold. When animals die, the producer, who paid no insurance premium and, in many cases, failed to protect animals from inclement weather, is rewarded with a government check for the deceased animals. LIP reimburses producers 75 percent of the dead animals' market value.

Working from government figures, I calculated that, in the previous five years, LIP had picked up the tab for a staggering three hundred thousand dead livestock and 7 million dead poultry. Likewise, in less than ten years, LIP had paid out more than $350,000,000 to producers. (Just imagine how far a third of a billion dollars could go if that money was used to enforce the federal Humane Methods of Slaughter Act!) *

Here's the kicker: While USDA is busy handing out our hard-earned taxpayer dollars to farmers and ranchers whose animals perished, that agency doesn't even require producers to provide the animals in their care with even the most basic protections from extreme weather. No shelter, shade, or other safeguards are mandated. In addition to rewarding producers for bad behavior, LIP represents misuse of taxpayer dollars and government waste at its most flagrant. In short, taxpayers are footing the bill for animal cruelty.**

In 2022, in a very reasonable request, HFA asked members of Congress to take action to ensure that farmers and ranchers receiving this government handout first put in place life-saving protections for their animals. This means developing and executing disaster preparedness plans for their livestock and poultry. These plans, we suggested, would have to be submitted to USDA before harsh weather struck and before compensation was made. In other words, no disaster plan, no reimbursement.

Responding to our request, an amazing fifty-one members of Congress stepped up to the plate.

"As the number of animal deaths and payments issued under LIP continue to increase each year," wrote members of Congress in a plea to the House Appropriations Committee, "we believe several concrete and commonsense reforms are needed to safeguard animal welfare, promote transparency, and ultimately save taxpayer dollars.

"The number of farm animals that die from adverse weather events is exceedingly large in scope," the members continued. "In 2018, approximately

---

* Between 2008 and 2024, LIP payments totaled more than $500,000,000.

** Disaster preparedness plans are already *recommended* by many livestock and poultry trade associations, including the National Chicken Council, National Turkey Federation, National Pork Board, and the North American Meat Institute.

Connecting the Dots 215

5.5 million poultry and [thousands of] pigs perished from hurricanes Florence and Michael alone. Winter storms resulted in the deaths of more than thirty-seven thousand cattle in Montana in the winter of 2018, and up to one hundred thousand beef cattle in South Dakota in 2013. In 2021, over one hundred thousand poultry in Louisiana died as a result of Hurricane Laura, and a deep freeze in Texas led to the deaths of hundreds of thousands of farm animals."

Reimbursing producers for dead animals without ever requiring that they provide safeguards from the elements, explained the congress members, "presents a clear disincentive for producers to take the necessary steps to implement disaster management plans and provide their animals with necessary protections."

At HFA's request, in 2023, Congressman Steve Cohen (D-TN) introduced in the US House of Representatives the "Emergency and Disaster Preparedness for Farm Animals Act." This legislation requires the development and execution of disaster plans by farmers and ranchers before they ever receive a dime of compensation under LIP. I'm thrilled to report that this is the first time that Congress has ever addressed LIP reform. While this bill is still in the process of moving through Congress, its future passage could help protect millions of animals, not to mention save taxpayers millions of dollars.

Chapter 59

There is no known cure for Visual Snow Syndrome. The only treatment is a single pharmaceutical that may provide some relief in a small minority of patients. That anti-seizure medication led to a slight improvement in five of twenty-six patients in a very limited trial—that was only 19 percent of those treated who benefitted at all.

Now that I had gotten to the bottom of what ailed me, I wanted to try that medication to see if it would work for me. With support and assistance from Dr. Goadsby and my local physician, I embarked on a several-month regimen of that drug.

I wish I could tell you that it worked, but it didn't.

That's okay. Now that I know what this disorder is, what is wrong with me, I also know what is right with me. I know that I'm not crazy or somehow to blame for my symptoms. That said, I can live with Visual Snow Syndrome.

After all, I had finally connected "the dots."

After fifty-four years of marriage, my mother moved out of my parents' home and divorced my father. My dad, eighty-two years old at the time, was nearly deaf—a remnant of his deployment as an airplane mechanic in the Army Air Force. He was also severely disabled with post-polio syndrome—a condition that affects polio survivors up to forty years after recovery from the dreaded disease and causes a constellation of nerve and muscular symptoms. Dad, once tall and imposing, now walked hunched over, first with two canes and then with a walker. Eventually he was relegated to a wheelchair. I was grateful I was more functional now and residing in Asheville, as I was able to support him as best as I could.

Connecting the Dots 217

Mom, now seventy-five and feeling liberated, ultimately bought an elegant condo with her boyfriend, a kind and caring man, and they moved in together. I was happy for my mother, but oh so heartbroken for my poor dad.

As for me, eventually I was able to leave my confining apartment behind. I purchased a new-construction house where my cat and I enjoyed the majority of our time on the spacious front screened porch and back deck. What a blessing to have my own special place, situated on an acre of mountain meadow and forest, where bear and turkey visitors came right up to my porch. Perhaps it wasn't the rugged beauty of the Montana Rockies, but the verdant Blue Ridge Mountains that enveloped my property were more approachable, more intimate, more welcoming to me. I was finally home.

Part Nine

The Meat Industry's Free Pass

Chapter 60

I will never forget the image of the frightened polar bear cubs on the PBS documentary—two white puff balls—on the ice floe, their bewildered eyes staring into the camera lens as their mother lay dying only feet away. But over the years, new images had been seared into my psyche.

Take, for example, the video I recently watched of agriculture authorities attempting to contain an outbreak of African swine fever (ASF) in China. African swine fever is a highly contagious viral hog disease that, as far as we know, does not affect humans.

The video showed pigs being pushed with a backhoe and forced to jump into a thirty-foot-deep pit. Landing on their former pen-mates, some sustained injuries in the fall. All were shrieking loudly.

Once the crater was filled with animals, the backhoe operator released a giant fireball down upon the pigs. It exploded like a bomb; the flames spread over the squealing victims in a second's time. Their desperate, shrill cries intensified—long and exaggerated screams—as their bodies burned. After a minute, the fire mercifully extinguished itself. As smoke arose from the charred, thrashing figures, their squeals continued, just at a reduced decibel level, accompanied by a few low groans.

Next, the backhoe operator began heaping dirt that had been excavated from the pit back into the mass grave, soil and rocks falling onto the hogs. As the animals were quickly buried alive, their screams became muffled, faint, and, soon, no more.[1]

It was the worst thing I'd ever seen.

When the African swine fever outbreak occurred in China from 2018 through 2021, many of the roughly *third of a billion* hogs destroyed there—a quarter of all the hogs in the world—were forced to jump into mass graves and buried alive. And, as the video revealed, some were actually set on fire before burial.

But why make an issue of this? Surely, such atrocities couldn't happen here in the United States.

Or *could* they?

In addition to Asia, African swine fever has infected hogs in Africa, Europe, and recently in North America, where it has been detected on farms in Haiti and the Dominican Republic, a stone's throw from the United States. Short of researchers developing a viable vaccine, if the disease were to touch down in our country, it would likely result in the extermination of millions of U.S. hogs.

"Depopulation" is the term animal agriculture has coined for the large-scale on-farm mass killing of animals who, due to disease or other unforeseen circumstances, such as natural or man-made disasters, can't be shipped to slaughter. The American Veterinary Medical Association (AVMA) defines it as "the rapid destruction of a population of animals in response to urgent circumstances with as much consideration given to the welfare of the animals *as practicable* [emphasis added]."[2] And, in the United States, we've seen depopulation methods so cruel they rival those utilized in China.

Coronavirus in the United States brought with it many tragedies, one of which was the spread of COVID-19 among slaughterhouse employees. Due to crowded conditions and lack of safeguards in packing plants, slaughterhouses became COVID hotspots; tens of thousands of employees became infected and hundreds died, resulting in the temporary closure of many large plants. Consequently, there was a tremendous backlog of farm animals destined for slaughter.

With the meat plants temporarily shuttered, just where were all those slaughter-bound animals supposed to go? I had an idea where they would end up. And my suspicion unfortunately proved to be true.

Many depopulation practices, though endorsed, at this book's press time, by the industry-biased American Veterinary Medical Association, are as diabolical as they are brutal. One common method of depopulating pigs

The Meat Industry's Free Pass   223

and poultry on farms occurs when producers simply seal up barn inlets, shut off ventilation system fans, heat the barn to triple digits and/or pump in added steam. The process is called "ventilation shutdown plus," the "plus" being the addition of heat or steam. And it's as cruel as it sounds.

Another AVMA-endorsed mechanism for depopulating chickens, pigs, and even cattle is the use of "water-based foam." The consistency of firefighting foam, this substance is sprayed inside barns or chambers, flowing up and over the panicked animals, suffocating or drowning them by occluding their airways.

There are less torturous ways to kill animals.

In the early months of COVID-19, when I learned that 2 million broiler chickens had quietly been depopulated in Delaware and Maryland due to bottlenecks at area slaughterhouses, I contacted a reporter at the *Washington Post*, providing her with all the information I had on both ventilation shutdown plus and water-based foam. "I am very concerned that the use of ventilation shutdown plus will not be limited to these 2 million birds," I wrote, "and, with slaughtering capacity dramatically down for market hogs, you can be sure that large numbers of hogs are being culled as we speak.

"People care about the inhumane treatment of farm animals," I continued, explaining to the reporter that our previous slaughterhouse story in the *Post* had generated an unprecedented reader response. "Somebody has to expose what is taking place behind the closed doors of pig and poultry operations."

The *Post* reported my facts, with quotes attributed to HFA, in an article exposing the impacts of the packinghouse closures.[3]

After that and other articles on the issue appeared, an undercover investigator documented on video hundreds of live pigs being subjected to ventilation shutdown plus at a large Iowa farm. Like their Chinese counterparts, these pigs shrieked vociferously as they, over a period of several hours, slowly died of hyperthermia—heat stroke. Water had been removed, so the pigs couldn't drink to cool down. They baked to death. Those who somehow managed to survive the assault overnight were rewarded the next morning with a blow to the head from a captive bolt gun.[4] In all, it is estimated that in one three-month period in 2020, veterinarians oversaw the destruction of roughly 243,000 pigs by ventilation shutdown plus, with a grand total of 1 million pigs being depopulated in that fashion that year.[5] My prediction to the *Post* regrettably had come true.

Likewise, between 2022 and early 2025, in an attempt to eradicate Highly Pathogenic Avian Influenza (a contagious virus that occurs mainly in birds but has now been detected in more than nine hundred dairy cow herds, as well as in numerous wild mammals, farmed mink, goats, cats, and even humans), USDA supervised the depopulation of laying hens, broiler chickens, turkeys, and ducks on commercial farms and in backyard flocks across the United States. When all was said and done, more than *150 million* birds—animals who had spent their lives confined in cramped battery cages and overcrowded warehouses—lay dead. The overwhelming majority of these birds were subjected to ventilation shutdown plus.[6]* At press time, the death toll was rising dramatically.

Again, our taxpayer dollars at work.

---

* The depopulations described here demonstrate the need for a massive overhaul of our food production system. Short of reform, however, there are less inhumane ways to kill animals on-farm than the default method of ventilation shutdown plus. Gassing animals in containers, partial houses, or whole houses with carbon dioxide is cruel—animals often exhibit head shaking, gasping, and attempts to escape—but death from the administration of CO_2 is considerably faster and the animals suffer less prior to losing consciousness than during barbaric ventilation shutdown plus. Conducting gassing with a mixture of nitrogen, argon, or other inert gases, is preferrable to CO_2, because pigs and poultry do not appear to be averse to these gases. Nitrogen-filled high expansion foam, in which animals die from anoxia, or lack of oxygen to the brain, is faster and less inhumane when compared to low- or medium-expansion water-based firefighting foam which kills animals by drowning or occlusion of the airways. While some depopulation methods are less brutal than others, all are a symptom of a food production system gone awry.

Chapter 61

When laws are passed, they're supposed to reflect the will of the people. In the last few decades, we've seen all fifty states in our country upgrade certain forms of animal cruelty to felony offenses. These laws are a moral statement that the American people wish to prevent animal cruelty. The public believes that animal abusers—whether they're individuals or corporations—should be prosecuted. And in those cases which are so egregious that they are classified as felonies, this means that criminals should be subject to fines in the tens of thousands of dollars' range, with maximum prison times being as long as ten years for each offense.

The depopulation methods I described, like the other offenses in this book, are clear violations of state anti-cruelty laws. Why then don't producers get prosecuted for their crimes? Why does the meat industry get a free pass? Because, for many years, agribusiness has operated outside the bounds of the law, chalking up its wrongdoings to the waste basket term "standard agricultural practices." There are no federal laws governing how farm animals are raised, and dozens of states exempt standard husbandry practices that are routinely performed on farm animals—such as tail docking and castration without anesthesia—from their cruelty laws. But, surely butchering, scalding, lynching, and baking live animals to death are not considered "standard agricultural practices." If someone would just enforce the law.

Sadly, as we've seen at the slaughterhouses, dairy, and hog farms we visited—with the exception of the last case where Special Prosecutor Frank Forchione stood his ground—prosecutorial discretion often subverts the will of the people. Prosecutorial discretion is so broad and so vague that it establishes a system whereby prosecutors can effectively ignore the law without any negative consequences.

Prosecutors are either appointed or elected to their posts. As a result, they may be beholden to those people who appointed them or who financially supported their elections. If they aspire to get reelected or to hold higher political offices—district attorneys often move up the ladder to become judges or seek other political positions—they look to their backers for future support. Likewise, attorneys general, either appointed by governors or elected, frequently have political ambitions.

Whether appointed or elected, local, state, and federal prosecutors are cognizant of their public images, often taking on cases that will bolster their careers and declining to prosecute those that could adversely affect them and their political prospects. For the record, this isn't a "red" or "blue" issue—Republican or Democrat—it happens across the board.

Washington's former Attorney General Christine Gregoire is a perfect case in point. She had the governorship in her crosshairs—a position she ultimately attained. As attorney general, Gregoire, a Democrat, was presented with overwhelming and irrefutable evidence that cows were being skinned alive at the IBP slaughterhouse. Instead of doing her job, she came up with a laundry list of reasons to not prosecute a large employer that contributed significantly to the state's coffers, and potentially to a gubernatorial campaign, and that represented one of the country's most powerful lobbies. After all, animals are not constituents, they have no standing in the justice system. As mentioned earlier, in the end, Washington's vote was one of the closest races in US election history, and certainly the tightest ever in that state. My guess is that, had she prosecuted IBP, she would not have become Governor Gregoire.

In each case described in this book, prosecutors were presented with overwhelming and irrefutable evidence that criminal offenses had taken place. And, in each instance, with the exception of the last one, self-interested prosecutors, at the behest of the meat industry, tried to shift blame and attack the whistleblowers.

So, there you have it. Ours may not be the most equitable justice system, but I guess it's the best justice system that we've got.

Part Ten

A Tearful Goodbye

Chapter 62

So, there I was in my pale-yellow gown and blue latex gloves, visiting Timothy Walker in the intensive care unit of Naples Community Hospital. Walker, as you will recall, was my very first whistleblower—the courageous man who I introduced you to at the beginning of this book who complained that live cows were having their heads skinned at Kaplan Industries in Florida.

Now, I knew that Tim had zero chance of outliving his nonsurvivable MRSA-infected wound.

The ventilator tube had been removed from his mouth two days earlier, and Tim, extremely weak, was somehow breathing on his own. He was no longer sedated; we had shared a few words the day before. But now, when we spoke to him, he could barely keep his eyes open. It took every ounce of energy for him to slightly lift his lids, and, after a second or two, his eyes would roll back a bit, and he would swiftly drift back to sleep.

It was now 2:00 p.m. and I had to catch my flight back to Asheville at four o'clock. I had two hours to make the fifty-minute drive to the Fort Myers airport, gas up, return the rental car, and arrive at the gate an hour before departure.

It was time to say goodbye.

It was my second trip to Florida this year to be with a dying friend. Six months earlier, I had been at the bedside of a dear friend suffering from brain cancer as she took her last breath. In addition to my parents, I had lost seven of my closest friends in the past few years and I had barely shed a tear.

Looking at the monitors surrounding him, and Tim lying so vulnerable in the hospital bed, his brother John leaning over him, and knowing that it was time to leave, I was suddenly overcome with grief. The woman who had suppressed her emotions for a lifetime finally let them flow.

I began sobbing silently, but apparently not softly enough. The nurse in the room got wind of my snuffling, and asked me if I needed a tissue. "Please," I implored in a whisper, as I stood next to the patient's bed. "Don't say anything. I don't want Tim to see me crying!"

With that, Tim suddenly bolted awake. He opened his big brown eyes—wide and clear—and gazed directly at me. Then he mumbled something under his breath that I couldn't quite make out.

I begged him to repeat himself and leaned in close to his lips. Whatever he said was inaudible again, and I couldn't grasp what he was trying to tell me. I was frustrated and panicked: did he need something to make him more comfortable? Was he trying to say goodbye? On the third try, I was, by the grace of God, able to understand exactly what he said.

The man who had been my friend for thirty years, my staunchest supporter and advocate, who was hanging onto life by a thread, looked me square in the eyes and simply said, "For the girl who worked in the projects."

I couldn't believe my ears.

In eight short words, Tim had just chided me for crying; taking me back to my work in the rundown Florida low-income housing project where I had tracked down the knocker from Kaplan Industries. Tim had often remarked how dangerous he thought that was. Timothy Walker, who had been barely conscious, had just shamed me for crying by reminding me how courageous *I* was.

I couldn't bear the tenderness of his comment.

With tears streaming down my cheeks, I simply said, "Tim, I love you so much." I walked to the door of the hospital room, stood for a moment—our eyes trained on each other—and then, as I got ready to leave, I blew him a kiss.

Lying in the hospital bed, his head on a white pillow, he mustered all of his energy and he firmly pursed his lips in return.

Out of the ICU I walked, stripping off the yellow gown and latex gloves, and made my way down the elevator to the ground floor ladies' room. Once there, I stood before a mirror and sobbed uncontrollably. I cried on the drive to the airport and in the terminal, and, as discreetly as possible, I wept on the plane all the way home.

Chapter 63

I've been going to Al-Anon—a twelve-step program—a few times a week for thirty years now. I've learned a lot in that program. As I said before, one of the greatest gifts of the program is the realization that I am not in control of the universe. I am not God. On the contrary, there is definitely something bigger than me out there.

I've seen it in the daily providential twists and turns that have happened along my path, of which I've named only a few in this book. For instance, had I not, as a teen, stumbled upon the PBS documentary on polar bears, I may never have pursued a career in animal protection. Had the exterminator not sprayed his insecticide directly over my baby bald eagle illustration, I may never have written for *The New York Times* or been hired by Christine Stevens, the "duchess of the defenseless." Had Timothy Walker's "anonymous" letter not landed in my inbox at HSUS, I may never have investigated slaughterhouses. Had unscrupulous David Wills not been appointed my immediate supervisor, I may never have left HSUS bound for HFA. Likewise, and most importantly, had a waterlogged natural sea sponge not broken in two, I might not have survived to tell my story. These things have changed the trajectory of my life for the better. Actually, for the best.

My twelve-step program has also taught me self-compassion. Since as long as I can remember, I've been empathetic toward others, but I had no consideration for myself. I'd blame myself for the slightest transgression, for not being perfect. Over and over, I'd beat myself up for my visual problem. Like a slaughterhouse worker wielding an electric prod.

In the program, gratitude has come naturally, and I've learned to let myself off the hook. I now understand that I'm not terminally unique and broken. Rather, I'm human, just another bozo on the bus. I am learning to love and accept myself exactly as I am.

And I no longer blame myself for my visual problem. Whereas I used to ask myself, "Why am I doing this to myself?" my new mantra is, "It never was your fault."

And I'm more in touch with my feelings now. I'll admit, not as much as I would like to be, but I'm getting there. After all, I did sob like a baby when I left Timothy Walker's side.

And that translates to the cruelty I've confronted as well.

When I wrote *Slaughterhouse*, I was detached, like an unfeeling observer, just uncovering and reporting the facts. My heart clamped shut, it was not safe to feel. But as time has marched on, I have come to acknowledge and internalize some of the abuses I've documented.

For example, I can't stop thinking about the nation's millions of breeding sows who are wrongfully convicted and sentenced to spend life inside crates where they can never turn around, not just now, not this day, not this night, not tomorrow morning, tomorrow afternoon, but next week, next month, and next year. Every time I think about them, they're still there. Immobilized. Traumatized. Each one a distinct but nameless individual with thoughts, feelings, personality traits, and pain of her own, a someone who no one knows, no one will ever know.

Nor will anyone contemplate or honor that particular being's suffering. Locked away in an endless cycle of impregnation, delivery, and separation from her offspring, a cycle that ends only when she collapses and is dragged from her crate by her snout or ears and is shot. Or is hanged. Or when she is tossed alive on a dead pile. If she is "salvageable" and makes it to the slaughterhouse, it will be her lucky day if she's actually rendered unconscious before she's bled and immersed in the scalding tank.

And yet, she has committed no crime, done nothing to offend. She just had the bad fortune to be born food. She can't know this is all for a bite of bacon.

Whereas my job was investigating and exposing before, my knowing now gnaws at my soul. I am haunted by the suffering of crated sows and dairy calves, the untold numbers of slaughter-bound creatures who are scalded, skinned, or dismembered alive, and the billions of other farm animals who are simply chewed up and spit out—or, in this case, actually devoured—by humans each year. Each and every one was a someone.

It bears mentioning that just as farm animals have the capacity to feel pain—after all, they have emotional processing centers in their brains similar to humans—they also have the potential to experience *pleasure*. When released, for instance, from intensive confinement to pasture, farm animals can often be observed running with abandon, kicking up their hooves, socializing, and playing. While it goes without saying, the overwhelming majority of farm animals, like those we've encountered in this book, are not afforded the opportunity to experience even one second of pleasure for the duration of their entire miserable lives.

It's estimated that the average hog factory farm puts ten family farmers out of business.[1] Thus, it's not surprising that these days, there are nearly twice as many people in prison as there are farmers in the United States.[2] Even so, through the use of technology, genetic engineering, and antibiotics which keep animals alive in the hostile, disease promoting conditions of factory farms, the number of creatures raised and slaughtered has skyrocketed. Fifty-five years ago, humans slaughtered just over ten billion farm animals annually worldwide.[3] Today, we kill about ten billion in the United States alone.[4] And we've exported our consumptive ways to emerging and developing countries, where economic development and urbanization have resulted in an astounding increase in meat consumption and corresponding slaughter. Globally, we slaughter more than eighty-two billion farm animals a year to feed our voracious appetites.[5]

For the advocates who have worked so hard to raise consciousness about the suffering endured by chickens, turkeys, ducks, and other birds, forgive me for not giving them their due in this book. I would be remiss not to mention poultry, who represent the majority of animals slaughtered in the United States, to the tune of more than nine and a half billion birds a year, or over three hundred birds a second. I do them justice in *Slaughterhouse,* describing the conditions under which they are raised and the dangers associated with eating contaminated poultry and poultry products. Bred for breast muscle or egg production and forced to grow faster or produce more eggs than their young bodies can bear, these birds suffer crippling deformities and production diseases that affect their respiratory, circulatory, muscular, and skeletal systems. You would think that images of broiler chickens, their legs splayed out under freakishly large bodies, and featherless laying hens crammed inside battery cages, would be enough to convince consumers to forgo the fast-food drive thru in favor of plant-based options.

And then there's their transport. Roughly 20 million chickens arrive dead at slaughterhouses annually in this country.[6] Perhaps they are the fortunate ones. After all, birds are not covered by the Humane Methods of Slaughter Act. As a result, most who survive the brutal journey to the slaughterhouse are violently shackled upside down by their fragile legs, have their heads dragged through an electrified water bath which shocks and immobilizes—but does not necessarily stun—them, have their throats partially cut, and then, after a brief bleed out, are immersed into the scalding tank, sometimes still alive and conscious.

Nor can we forget the fishes. The figures above are dwarfed by the inordinate number of fishes consumed. The cruelty we inflict on sentient fishes merits an entire book of its own. Each year the multibillion-dollar fishing industry uses longlines, gillnets, and trawlers—in which massive nets are dragged along the ocean floor—to catch trillions of fish, not to mention indiscriminate species or "bycatch" such as birds, dolphins, sea turtles, seals, and even whales. More than 100 billion farmed fishes, confined in crowded pens that are polluted with feces and decomposing feed, experience parasitic outbreaks requiring the heavy use of antibiotics and other chemicals. Fishes' ultimate deaths from suffocation, chilling, carbon dioxide, or bleeding are inhumane, to say the least.

As I write this, I'm sitting on an airplane, where I have been reading yet another Holocaust memoir. I have become a voracious reader of books about the Holocaust. Each book I read about the gratuitous and methodical

A Tearful Goodbye 235

brutality followed only by death that human beings deliberately inflicted on their fellows, I am horrified and aghast. Yet, reading these books enables me to better understand how farm and slaughterhouse managers can support, supervise and, in some cases, perpetrate the premeditated and systematic cruelty I've documented against the most vulnerable among us—helpless animals. And how, for the rest of society, ignorance is bliss. Unbeknownst to most consumers and subsidized by them, the silent annihilation continues unabated.

I've held these accounts close for a few years now. It helps me to share them with you. Perhaps because of the isolation and alienation I experienced due to my OCD and visual problem, I relate to the isolation and alienation that farm animals experience in our society.

The one thing I know for sure is that I can no longer close my eyes—*or my heart*—to their suffering. Now that you know, neither can you.

Afterword
A Heartfelt Plea

The dog's name is Dexter. He's a bicolor Brittany Spaniel living in the Rocky Mountain town of Ouray, Colorado. When Dexter was a puppy, he escaped his home, darted into traffic, and was hit by a vehicle. He lost one front leg and badly injured the other. So, remarkably, he taught himself to walk upright on his two hind legs. When he goes out for walks with his person, he resembles a furry little human strolling down the street.

According to a report on the *CBS Evening News*, "In the six years since [his accident], Dexter has become a full-blown celebrity, starring in parades and building a legion of social media followers, who now come to the dog's hometown from across the country just hoping for a glimpse of Ouray's most upstanding citizen. In a pile of mail he receives monthly are hundreds of letters of heartfelt gratitude."[1]

His fans are apparently inspired by Dexter's ingenuity, adaptability, and resilience. I get that. It is indeed inspiring that a little dog could overcome such loss. But I also think that people connect with Dexter because he walks erect like a human. He's very relatable.

I like the Dexter story, because I think it drives home the point that most people compartmentalize animals in their minds. There's one place in their brains for companion animals, meaning dogs and cats, another for the farm animals who they eat.

In reality, the cognitive dissonance that exists in the minds of many people, when it comes to the difference between pets and farm animals, is stunning. Perhaps if farm animals bi-pedaled down the parade route like humans, maybe they, too, would be celebrated. And receive fan mail.

Unfortunately, they don't. And so, they are subjected to the abuses you've just read about.

It's not only pets like Dexter who are resilient and sociable. There are countless videos online depicting people playing fetch with cows, pigs, goats, sheep, and even chickens. Others show humans greeting farm animals only to have them come rushing in for an embrace. In one touching video, a group of trombone players entices an entire herd of cattle to come listen. In another, a ukelele player serenades a besotted donkey.

Cows are very complicated creatures. They develop strong and lasting social bonds with herd mates and usually have between two and four close friends. They prefer cows their own age or those with whom they've been raised,[2] and make friendships for life. Their relationships are devoted, not casual. Cows communicate by staring,[3] and they have excellent memories—remembering at least fifty bovine and ten human faces for several years.[4] When split from their offspring, they call out for their calves for, in some cases, days. They rapidly move back and forth in their enclosures in an attempt to reunite, or when possible, chase after trailers that are transporting their calves away.

Pigs are by nature highly intelligent, rambunctious, complex, and very inquisitive. Pigs on pasture have been known to gather up food and bring it to injured siblings. Pigs are arguably smarter than dogs. One pig enthusiast said that her pet pig would "come when called, sit, kiss, kneel, play the toy piano, and open the fridge if she gets half a chance."[5] And, according to a story in *The New York Times*, "Pigs are among the quickest of animals to learn a new routine and pigs can do a circus' worth of tricks: jump hoops, bow and stand, spin, and make word-like sounds on command . . . herd sheep, close and open cages, play video games with joysticks, and more."[6]

Whether they be cows, pigs, chickens, turkeys, ducks, goats, or sheep, all farm animals are endowed with complex thoughts, social skills, innate emotions, instincts, intuition, the capacity for affection, need I go on?

If Dexter the dog's devotees only knew and cared about the capacities and fates of his brethren. . .

Afterword: A Heartfelt Plea 239

My objective in writing this book was to help readers—and perhaps, in so doing, enable *myself*—to move past the denial, numbness, and self-protection that prevent so many from confronting the truth about farm animal abuse. Since the animals can't speak for themselves, I've tried to bring them to life for you, to make them as relatable as Dexter the dog. My goal is to encourage empathy and understanding. You've already demonstrated your empathy and your courage by simply reading my words.

In an interview[7] about her compelling memoir *The Choice*—a tale of one young woman's death-defying struggle at Auschwitz—Dr. Edith Eva Eger recalled the one question that haunted her most deeply while surviving in the extermination camp. Both parents dead, she wondered, "Does anyone know I'm here?" The isolation and alienation were staggering.

And that question translates to farm animals, as well. Now that I, and hopefully others, are becoming more aware, we can finally contemplate the isolation and alienation experienced by those defenseless beings raised and slaughtered for food. I wish the animals I've written about, and countless billions of others, could know, on some universal level, that someone, somewhere, was mourning their pitiful lives and violent deaths, crying for those in factory farms and slaughterhouses.

"Does anyone know we're here?"

Yes, we know. We've heard and we've listened. We know you are there.

Please use the information below to help effect change on behalf of farm animals:

To support HFA's campaign against factory farming and slaughterhouse abuses, please visit www.hfa.org.

Please ask your members of Congress to support the Save America's Forgotten Equines (SAFE) Act. Congress has defunded horse slaughter inspections for human consumption, temporarily shutting down horse slaughter in the United States. However, tens of thousands of horses endure untold suffering as they are trucked to Mexico and Canada to be killed. The SAFE Act would both permanently ban horse slaughter in the United States and prohibit the export of horses for slaughter.

Also, please urge your members of Congress to support the Emergency and Disaster Preparedness for Farm Animals Act. Tell your lawmakers to require that livestock producers develop and execute disaster-preparedness plans before they ever receive federal compensation for dead animals under the USDA's Livestock Indemnity Program (LIP).

> *For contact information for your federal legislators,*
> *go to www.congress.gov/members/find-your-member*
> *or call the Capitol switchboard at (202) 224–3121.*

Finally, contact the American Veterinary Medical Association (AVMA) and demand that its members stop endorsing cruel ventilation shutdown plus, water-based foam, and blunt-force trauma (thumping of piglets) for farm animal "depopulation."

> *Submit comments at www.avma.org/about/contact or at*
> *AVMA, 1931 North Meacham Road, Suite 100, Schaumburg,*
> *IL 60173–4360.*

Thank you.

Afterword: A Heartfelt Plea 241

The Humane Farming Association (HFA)

The Humane Farming Association (HFA) is dedicated to the protection of farm animals and operates the largest farm-animal sanctuary in the United States. Founded in 1985, HFA is nationally recognized for its groundbreaking anti-cruelty campaigns.

HFA's goals are: 1) to protect farm animals from cruelty; 2) to protect the public from dangerous misuse of antibiotics, hormones, and other chemicals used on factory farms; and 3) to protect the environment from the impacts of industrialized animal factories.

HFA's programs include anti-cruelty investigations and exposés, national media campaigns, humane education, and legislative efforts on behalf of farm animals. HFA also operates Suwanna Ranch, a seven-thousand-acre refuge located in Northern California, where it provides emergency hands-on care for, and permanent homes to, more than one thousand rescued farm animals.

Acknowledgments

When I began writing this book, I knew that I had difficulty processing visual information, but I didn't know what disorder I suffered from. Amazingly, a definitive diagnosis wouldn't come until I was about halfway through writing my manuscript. That said, I couldn't have written this book without the support of many.

The love of my sister, Lisa, brother-in-law, Bob, and their family—Jessica, Asher, Amanda, and Zia—as well that of as my treasured tabby cat, sustained and nourished me every day and every step of the way in writing this book, and continues to do so today. Without them, I would be nowhere.

Although no longer with us, my parents, Phyllis and Gerald, did their very best to both help me solve and cope with my mysterious disorder over the years. To them, and to the many others whom I have lost along the way, you are my angels.

My cherished friends—you know who you are—have been an endless source of encouragement and, of course, joy. I am so wealthy with friends. And, my gratitude for my friendships extends to my compassionate Al-Anon sponsor, Judy.

To Suzanne Fix, my former counselor and current friend, who listened intently to my stories and suggested that they were worthy of a book, herein lies the fruit of your suggestion. I thank you.

I am indebted to HFA National Director Bradley Miller, without whose patience, understanding, and support this book would not have seen the light of day.

Thank you, Jonathan Balcombe, PhD, for generously taking the time necessary to review my words and provide invaluable feedback.

Sincere thanks go to Skyhorse Publisher Tony Lyons and Skyhorse Executive Editor Daniela Rapp for their fervent stance against censorship and their willingness to take a risk on a very controversial subject. I am in Daniela's debt for her discerning, painstaking, and thoughtful nurturance of my manuscript, and her passion for and dedication to exposing injustices to animals.

And finally, my heartfelt appreciation goes to all the heroic, inspiring whistleblowers who risked their livelihoods to go on record on audio and videotape, and ultimately in this book, with shocking revelations about what takes place inside America's slaughterhouses and factory farms. You have demonstrated courage beyond words. That includes you, Timothy Walker, wherever you may be. I suspect that would be heaven. You have indeed earned your wings.

Endnotes

Chapter 3

1 *Say Goodbye,* Films Incorporated, Quaker Oats, Public Broadcasting System, 1972, television broadcast, www.youtube.com/watch?v=U8yo9PlFWAY.
2 UN Report, "Nature's Dangerous Decline 'Unprecedented'; Species Extinction Rates 'Accelerating'," May 6, 2019, www.un.org/sustainabledevelopment/blog/2019/05/nature-decline-unprecedented-report/.
3 "Almost One in Four Mammal Species Threatened with Extinction," European Commission, CORDIS, EU Research Results. March 2, 2023, accessed April 23, 2024, https://cordis.europa.eu/article/id/29941-almost-one-in-four-mammal-species-threatened-with-extinction#:~:text=Approximately%20one%20in%20four%20species,(International%20Union%20for%20.

Chapter 7

1 "New Jersey's Bald Eagle Population Continue to Climb, With 250 Active Nests Identified in 2022," New Jersey Department of Environmental Protection news release, January 20, 2023, access date December 21, 2023, www.nj.gov/dep/newsrel/2023/23_0004.htm.
2 Gail Ann Eisnitz, "The Eagle and the Exterminator," *New York Times,* August 22, 1982, www.nytimes.com/1982/08/22/nyregion/speaking-personally-the-eagle-and-the-exterminator.html.

Chapter 8

1 Gail Ann Eisnitz, "Is the Veal Calf Being Mistreated?," *New York Times,* July 17, 1983, www.nytimes.com/1983/07/17/nyregion/is-the-veal-calf-being-mistreated.html.

Chapter 9

1 Gail Ann Eisnitz, "Leg-Hold Traps Should Be Banned," *New York Times,* December 11, 1983, www.nytimes.com/1983/12/11/nyregion/leghold-traps-should-be-banned.html.
2 Gail Eisnitz, "Owners Reclaim Stolen Dogs from Mayo's," *The Animal Welfare Institute Quarterly,* Spring, 1984.

OUT OF SIGHT

Chapter 11

1 Paul A. Engelmayer, "Infiltrating Dogfight and Cockfight Rings Takes Guile and Guts," *Wall Street Journal*, March 2, 1984.

2 Arline and Harold Brecher, "Over 150,000 Horribly Abused at Auctions—Crippled, Sick, and Starving," *National Enquirer*, April 10, 1990.

Chapter 14

1 "Worker Exposes Inhumane Slaughter," *The Animals' Voice*, Volume 2, Number 5, 1989, p. 57.

Chapter 18

1 Tracy Thompson, "The Fur is Flying at the Humane Society," *Washington Post*, August 14, 1996, https://washingtonpost.com/archive/politics/1996/08/14 /fur-is-flying-at-the-humane-society/193d8364-b3aa-4f5c-8d4b-0eeb07460aa8/.

Chapter 21

1 Marian Burros, "Veal to Love, Without the Guilt," *New York Times*, April 18, 2007, www.nytimes.com/2007/04/18/dining/18veal.html.

Chapter 23

1 Danielle Paquette, "The Humane Society's Sexual Harassment Scandal Just Won't End," *Washington Post*, March 23, 2018, www.washingtonpost.com/business /economy/the-humane-societys-sexual-harassment-scandal-just-wont-end/2018 /03/23/52b8e996–1647-11e8–8b08–027a6ccb38eb_story.html.

2 Compiled from reports by staff writers Michael E. Ruane, Craig Whitlock, Ruben Castaneda, Patricia Davis, and Tom Jackman, "Humane Society Investigator Pleads Guilty," Crime and Justice, *Washington Post*, June 16, 1999, www .washingtonpost.com/archive/local/1999/06/17/crime-and-justice/900aff04 –930d-4972–9fe0-f9552703bb4d/.

3 United States Attorney's Office, Southern District of Texas, "Jury Convicts Local Businessman of Long-Term Sex Trafficking of Minor," press release, October 8, 2019, www.justice.gov/usao-sdtx/pr/jury-convicts-local-businessman -long-term-sex-trafficking-minor.

Chapter 24

1 Opinion Editor Myron B. Pitts, "If A Smithfield Pig Was Shot While Conscious Like PETA Says, What Happens Next?" *Fayetteville Observer*, August 15, 2024, www.fayobserver.com/story/opinion/2024/08/15/peta-smithfield-pig-usda-fsis /74776679007/.

2 Erica Shaffer, "Epic Assembly at Smithfield's Tar Heel Plant," *Meat + Poultry*, October 11, 2023, www.meatpoultry.com/articles/29176-epic-assembly.

Chapter 25

1 Daniel P. Puzo, "Probe Links Toxic Drug to Some Veal Producers," *Los Angeles Times*, October 14, 1994, www.latimes.com/archives/la-xpm-1994–10-14-mn -50292-story.html.

Chapter 30

1 Sam Verhovek, "Meat-Plant Workers Are the Latest Example of Immigrants Packing the Picket Lines," *New York Times*, June 26, 1999, www.nytimes.com/1999/06/26/us/meat-plant-workers-are-the-latest-example-of-immigrants-packing-the-picket-lines.html.

Chapter 32

1 Eli Sanders, "Workers Accuse Slaughterhouse of Animal Cruelty," *Seattle Times*, June 1, 2000, http://community.seattletimes.nwsource.com/archive/?date=20000601&slug=4023993.

2 Jim Lynch, "Washington is Investigating the IBP Meatpacking Plant After a Secretly Shot Video Shows Cows Kicking While Being Butchered," *Oregonian*, January 24, 2001, http://nobull.mikecallicrate.com/2002/01/24/washington-is-investigating-the-ibp-meatpacking-plant-after-a-secretly-shot-video-shows-cows-kicking-while-being-butchered/.

3 "Monday's Wash, Local," *Walla Walla Union Bulletin*, January 7, 2000, p.7.

4 Eli Sanders, "Judge Dismisses Lawsuit Over Washington Election," *New York Times*, June 7, 2005, www.nytimes.com/2005/06/07/us/judge-dismisses-lawsuit-over-washington-election.html.

Chapter 34

1 Joby Warrick, Melanie Sill, and Pat Stith, "Boss Hog: The Power of Pork, North Carolina's Pork Revolution" (series of nine articles), *Raleigh News & Observer*, February 19–29, 1995, www.pulitzer.org/winners/news-observer-raleigh-nc.

2 Joby Warrick, "They Die Piece by Piece; Modern Meat, Brutal Harvest," *Washington Post*, April 10, 2001, p.1. www.washingtonpost.com/archive/politics/2001/04/10/they-die-piece-by-piece/f172dd3c-0383–49f8-b6d8–347e04b68da1/.

3 Speech by Senator Robert Byrd, *Washington Journal, CSPAN 2*, July 9, 2001.

4 Government Accountability Office, "USDA Has Addressed Some Problems but Still Faces Enforcement Challenges," January, 2004:GAO-04–247, p.16.

5 Dena Jones, "Humane Slaughter Update, Federal and State Oversight of the Welfare of Farm Animals at Slaughter," Animal Welfare Institute, April 2020, 20HumaneSlaughterUpdate.pdf (awionline.org), p. 1.

Chapter 37

1 Otto M. Radostits, Clive C. Gay, Kenneth W. Hinchcliff, Peter D. Constable (eds), *Veterinary Medicine: A textbook of diseases of cattle. Horses, sheep, pigs, and goats* (United Kingdom, Elsevier Health Sciences, 2006).

Chapter 38

1 Melody Petersen, "Indians Now Disdain a Farm Once Hailed for Giving Tribe Jobs," *New York Times*, November 15, 2003, www.nytimes.com/2003/11/15/us/indians-now-disdain-a-farm-once-hailed-for-giving-tribe-jobs.html.

248   OUT OF SIGHT

2   Joe Kafka, "Attorney General Dismisses Animal Abuse Allegations." Associated Press, *Rapid City Journal*, July 27, 2004, http://rapidcityjournal .com/news/state-and-regional/ag-dismisses-allegations-of-hog-farm-abuse /article_7769e479-bd5b-550a-bd30-418493fb7c44.html.

Chapter 39

1   Emily Langer, "Doctor of 'Awakenings' and Poet Laureate of Medicine, Dies at 82," *Washington Post*, August 30, 2015, www.washingtonpost.com/national /health-science/oliver-sacks-doctor-of-awakenings-and-poet-laureate-of-medicine -dies-at-82/2015/08/30/62ba620c-4f0c-11e5-933e-7d06c647a395_story.html.

2   Israel Rosenfeld, "Like Dreams or Stupors," *New York Times*, July 7, 1985, www .nytimes.com/1985/07/07/books/like-dreams-or-stupors.html.

Chapter 41

1   Andrew Martin, "At Some Farms, It's 'Hog Hell,'" *Chicago Tribune*, March 24, 2004, www.chicagotribune.com/2004/03/24/at-some-farms-its-hog-hell/.

2   Donald L. Bartlett and James B. Steele, "The Empire of the Pigs: A Little-Known Company is a Master at Milking Governments for Welfare," *Time*, November 30, 1998, p. 60, https://content.time.com/time/magazine/article/0,9171,140572,00 .html.

3   Bartlett and Steele, "The Empire of the Pigs," p. 60.

4   Vicki Fecteau, Canadian coalition for Farm Animals, email to Gail Eisnitz, https: //preventingbarnfires.com/English/Barn%20Fires.pdf, April 27, 2023.

5   "Barn Fires," *Animal Welfare Institute,* access date April 18, 2024, https://awion line.org/content/barn-fires.

Chapter 51

1   Bill Lilley, "Group's Ad Stirs Up Emotions; Readers Flood Prosecutor with Calls, E-mails about Alleged Abuse on Pig Farm," *Akron Beacon Journal*, December 17, 2006.

2   "Ohio Pig Farmer Charged with Animal Cruelty," *WTOL-TV 11*, January 17, 2007.

3   Bill Lilley, "Pig Farm Employee, Owners Charged, Animal Group that Publicized Creston Operation Says Ohio Should Toughen Laws," *Akron Beacon Journal*, January 17, 2007.

4   Shane Hoover, "Charges Filed Over Alleged Abuse of Pigs," *Canton Repository*, January 17, 2007.

5   Zach Bolinger, "Supporters Join Together to Help Family Farm," *Wooster Daily Record*, June 17, 2007, www.the-daily-record.com/story/news/2007/06/17/ supporters-join-together-to-help/19484649007/.

Chapter 56

1   Andrea Zippay, "Ohio Pork Producers Help Wiles Farm," *Farm and Dairy*, August 9, 2007, www.farmanddairy.com/news/ohio-pork-producers-help-wiles-farm/901 .html.

Endnotes 249

2   Andrea Zippay, "Farmers: Look, Listen and Then Talk," *Farm and Dairy*, March 15, 2007, www.farmanddairy.com/news/farmers-look-listen-and-then-talk.

Chapter 57

1   "Visual Snow Syndrome," National Organization for Rare Disorders Rare Disease Database, May 31, 2018, access date August 8, 2020, https://rarediseases.org/rare-diseases/visual-snow-syndrome/.

2   "Disrupted Connectivity within Visual, Attentional and Salience Networks in the Visual Snow Syndrome," Eye on Vision Foundation, August 6, 2021, access date October 6, 2021, www.eyeonvision.org/research—news/disrupted-connectivity-within-visual-attentional-and-salience-networks-in-the-visual-snow-syndrome.

3   Colleen Doherty, MD, "What Is Visual Snow Syndrome, This Rare Condition is Not a Type of Migraine," Verywell Health, August 28, 2023, access date September 28, 2023, Visual Snow Syndrome: Symptoms, Causes, Treatment (verywellhealth.com).

4   Caroline Seydel, "Peter Goadsby, Migraine Expert, Awarded the Brain Prize 2021," UCLA Newsroom, March 4, 2021, https://newsroom.ucla.edu/dept/faculty/peter-goadsby-migraine-expert-awarded-brain-prize-2021.

Chapter 60

1   "Pigs Burned Alive in China; How Meat Farms are Killing Pigs in China," *Kinder World*, December 2018, access date December 15, 2019, www.kinderworld.org/videos/meat-industry/pigs-burned-alive-china/.

2   "AVMA Guidelines for the Depopulation of Animals, 2019 Edition," American Veterinary Medical Association, access date April 18, 2024, www.avma.org/sites/default/files/resources/AVMA-Guidelines-for-the-Depopulation-of-Animals.pdf.

3   Laura Reiley, "In One Month, The Meat Industry's Supply Chain Broke. Here's What You Need to Know," *Washington Post*, April 28, 2020, www.washingtonpost.com/business/2020/04/28/meat-industry-supply-chain-faq/.

4   Glenn Greenwald, "Hidden Video and Whistleblower Reveal Gruesome Mass-Extermination Method for Iowa Pigs Amid Pandemic, Pigs are Being Slowly Suffocated and Roasted to Death by an Agriculture Industry That Relies on Secrecy," *The Intercept*, May 29, 2020, access date, June 1, 2020, www.theintercept.com/2020/05/29/pigs-factory-farms-ventilation-shutdown-coronavirus/.

5   Peter Singer, *Animal Liberation Now: The Definitive Classic Renewed*, New York, Harper Perennial, 2023, pp. 107–108.

6   "Brownley Leads Bipartisan Effort to Urge More Humane Depopulation Methods of Affected Animals in Outbreak Mitigation," Congresswoman Julia Brownley Press Release, February 14, 2024, access date February 15, 2024, https://juliabrownley.house.gov/brownley-leads-bipartisan-effort-to-urge-more-humane-depopulation-methods-of-affected-animals-in-outbreak-mitigation/.

Chapter 63

1　Daneil Imhoff, editor, *The CAFO Reader, The Tragedy of Industrial Animal Factories*, Foundation for Deep Ecology in collaboration with Watershed Media, 2010, p. 64.

2　Joel Salatin, contributor, *The CAFO Reader, The Tragedy of Industrial Animal Factories*, Foundation for Deep Ecology in collaboration with Watershed Media, 2010, p. 357.

3　"Yearly number of Animals Slaughtered for Meat, World, 1961 to 2022," *Our World in Data*, access date February 10, 2024, www.ourworldindata.org/grapher /animals-slaughtered-for-meat?time=earliest..2022.

4　"Yearly Number of Animals Slaughtered for Meat, United States, 1961 to 2022." *Our World in Data*, access date February 10, 2024, www.ourworldindata.org /grapher/animals-slaughtered-for-meat?country=~USA.

5　Yearly number of Animals Slaughtered for Meat, World, 1961 to 2022," *Our World in Data*, access date February 10, 2024, www.ourworldindata.org/grapher /animals-slaughtered-for-meat?time=earliest..2022

6　Sophie Kevany, "More Than 20 Million Farm Animals Die On Way to Abattoir in US Every Year," *The Guardian*, June 15, 2022, www.theguardian.com/environment /2022/jun/15/more-than-20-million-farm-animals-die-on-way-to-abattoir-in-us -every-year.

Afterword

1　Steve Hartman,"Meet the Dog Who Learned to Walk Like a Human, On the Road With Steve Hartman," *CBS News*, July 8, 2022, www.cbsnews.com/video /meet-the-dog-who-learned-to-walk-like-a-human/.

2　Amy Hatkoff, *The Inner World of Farm Animals: Their Amazing Social, Emotional, and Intellectual Capacities*, Stewart, Tabori & Chang, 2009, p. 64.

3　Marc Bekoff, PhD, "Dead Cow Walking: The Case Against Born-Again Carnivorism," *The Atlantic*, December 27, 2011, www.theatlantic.com/health/archive/2011/12 /dead-cow-walking-the-case-against-born-again-carnivorism/250506/.

4　Amy Hatkoff, *The Inner World of Farm Animals: Their Amazing Social, Emotional, and Intellectual Capacities*, Stewart, Tabori & Chang, 2009, p. 72.

5　Amy Hatkoff, *The Inner World of Farm Animals*, p. 98.

6　Natalie Angier, "Pigs Prove to Be Smart, if Not Vain," *The New York Times Science Section*, November 9, 2009, www.nytimes.com/2009/11/10/science/10angier.html.

7　Super Soul Sunday, "Dr. Edith Eva Eger: We Choose to Be Victims," original air date June 24, 2019, www.oprah.com/own-super-soul-sunday/dr-edith-eva-eger -we-choose-to-be-victims.